KW-225-059

J. M. Loughridge

May 20th. 1992.

THE CROWN OF SONG

The Crown of Song
Metaphor in Pindar

Deborah Steiner

Duckworth

First published in 1986 by
Gerald Duckworth & Co. Ltd.
The Old Piano Factory
43 Gloucester Crescent, London NW1

© 1986 by Deborah Steiner

All rights reserved. No part of this publication
may be reproduced, stored in a retrieval system, or
transmitted, in any form or by any means, electronic,
mechanical, photocopying, recording or otherwise,
without the prior permission of the publisher.

ISBN 0 7156 2079 7

British Library Cataloguing in Publication Data

Steiner, Deborah
    The crown of song: metaphor in Pindar.
    1. Pindar—Criticism and interpretation
    2. Metaphor
    I. Title
    884'.01   PA4276

    ISBN 0-7156-2079-7

Photoset in North Wales by
Derek Doyle & Associates, Mold, Clwyd
Printed in Great Britain by
Redwood Burn Limited, Trowbridge

Contents

Preface ix
Abbreviations xiii

1. Theories of Metaphor, Ancient and Modern 1
2. Pindaric Metaphor, Function and Form 18
3. Of Plants and Men 28
4. Truth and Beauty 40
5. Craftsmanship 52
6. The Winds and Waves 66
7. Pindar's Paths 76
8. Landscape 87
9. Birds and Beasts 99
10. The Athletic Metaphor 111
11. Intimations of Immortality 122
12. Between Myth and Metaphor 136

Epilogue 149
Bibliography 154
Index 161

For Storm Jameson

Preface

Much of Pindar is lost to us. His epinician odes celebrate victors in athletic competitions which share nothing with today's Olympics beyond a name. It is impossible to recreate the elements of music and dance that were integral to many of the songs, and attempts to re-enact the ceremonies where they were performed would be artificial at best. This book, then, is concerned with what does remain, the text itself, and with the language that makes it live in modern ears. If Pindar is remote from us in genre, his style strikes the reader as vivid and immediate. And, in my reading of the epinician odes, it is the poet's use of metaphor that accounts for the dynamic quality of his verse.

There are many ways of approaching metaphor, of analysing it according to symbol, theme or grammar. Each category I select could be, and in some cases has been, the subject of an entire work. Each symbol has a history of its own, one that frequently stretches from Vedic and Homeric texts to the poetry that appears today. Within a poet's work, a symbol may evolve and change, and some would argue that counting and classifying metaphors provides a key to the development of the particular author. These subjects lie outside the immediate scope of this book, which examines just some of the metaphors that fill Pindar's odes to bursting point. In selecting the motifs I explore, I hope to include both those that the poet himself repeatedly evokes and those that seem to express Pindar's own understanding of his craft and of the role that it plays within the lives of men.

The particular demands of encomiastic verse, which belonged to a recognised tradition and had to satisfy the demands of the patrons for whom it was composed, in part dictated Pindar's choice of imagery. He favoured metaphors that lent themselves to the structure of the epinician ode, and allowed him to introduce the elements the genre required. Because of the distinctive nature of the victory song, I have restricted this study to the odes themselves, neglecting the rest of Pindar's choral poetry, his hymns, dithyrambs, laments and other songs which merit more attention than they have received. These too are rich in metaphors, many similar in type to those found in the odes, expressing similar concerns. In focusing on the odes, I had the benefit of a relatively sound text, and all quotations are taken from the excellent Teubner edition by B. Snell and revised by H. Maehler.

Selecting one feature of the text, and a purely literary one at that, risks banishing the author and his historical context from the scene. Those who prefer to read their Pindar rooted in his time and place will find an absence of references to the actual people and historical events that lie behind many of his metaphors. It is, of course, helpful to know if a particular battle suggested an image of a storm of blood, or a rival poet a metaphor of animal behaviour. Fortunately the background to the odes has been amply researched elsewhere, and the language combed for clues to the biography of the poet and those for whom he wrote. My defence for the approach this book adopts is that Pindar chose to portray the actual in metaphor, and the reader may respect his choice.

Why Pindar found in metaphor the means of expressing his concerns is the broader question this work touches on. I have looked at the problem first from the viewpoint of the scholars and critics who have examined verbal figuration, and then from the angle of the poet himself. The role that metaphor plays in poetry is different, I believe, from its function in everyday spech. I attempt to show that it can address questions which lie beyond the scope of literal language, and that these are the questions to which the poet returns. The poet is the supreme maker of metaphors precisely because the medium in which he writes has something of the fantastical about it, notably the power of living on even after the death of the author and his subject. One intriguing question that remains is why poets return so obstinately to the same images: which came first, the symbol, or the idea of perennial concern that it expresses? Certainly the poet's instinctive understanding of the power of symbolic language predates attempts by scholars and linguists to pin down its elusive quality. Writing about metaphor is a little like chasing one's own tail; it is impossible to discuss except through other metaphors.

It only remains for me to thank the people who have helped me in my work. My teachers of Greek at Harvard, particularly Albert Henrichs, provided the motivation and the means for me to go to Oxford where the book was written. My tutor there, Hugh Lloyd-Jones, was unfailing in the scholarship and encouragement he supplied. Many thanks are also due to Oliver Taplin, Mary Lefkowitz, Nicholas Richardson, Margaret Howatson and to Donald Carne-Ross whose essay on Pindar's sixth Olympian unwittingly planted the seed of my interest in the poet.

D.S.

Abbreviations

Ancient authors and works

Homer

Il. *Iliad*
Od. *Odyssey*

Pindar

Fr. Fragment
I. *Isthmian*
N. *Nemean*
O. *Olympian*
P. *Pythian*

All references are to the Teubner text edited by B. Snell and revised by H. Maehler (vol. 1 1984, vol. 2 1975).

Journals

AJPh *American Journal of Philology*
BSA *Annual of the British School at Athens*
CQ *Classical Quarterly*
CR *Classical Review*
GRBS *Greek, Roman and Byzantine Studies*
HSCP *Harvard Studies in Classical Philology*
JHS *Journal of Hellenic Studies*
MH *Museum Helveticum*
PBA *Proceedings of the British Academy*
QUCC *Quaderni Urbinati di Cultura Classica*
REG *Revue des Etudes Grecques*
REL *Revue des Etudes Latins*

Abbreviations

RPh	*Revue de philologie, de littérature et d'histoire anciennes*
TAPA	*Transactions and Proceedings of the American Philological Association*
YCS	*Yale Classical Studies*
ZPE	*Zeitschrift für Papyrologie und Epigraphik*

1

Theories of Metaphor, Ancient and Modern

Metaphor existed long before it became the object of critical study. It is a vital part of any living language which must constantly find terms for new elements without an infinite multiplication of vocabulary. Metaphors attach themselves to novel discoveries and newly identified phenomena; through metaphor we attribute 'channels' to televisions and 'stations' to radios. Metaphor is a device of thought as well as language, serving as an economical means of joining the dense and speculative to what is known and available in ordinary speech. Its range in both classical and modern times within the realm of thoughts and ideas is almost limitless, covering philosophical, metaphysical and scientific concepts which defy direct representation. Metaphoric thinking lies behind descriptions of natural phenomena which portray the sun, earth, sky and sea as living forces, possessing a will of their own. The Greeks made of the earth, its genesis and evolution, a living organism, the home of the gods who directed its motions. The realms of the arts and crafts in ancient and more modern times have generated vocabulary for the functioning of the world, and for those of its properties which escape clear scientific account. The same terminology applies to more human concerns, describing the working of such intangibles as fate and fortune which weave and spin their devices about the lives of mortal men. Another elusive concept is the human soul with its rapid emotions and desires. Metaphor can portray not only its behaviour, but the paradoxical nature of the feelings it entertains. Metaphor alone may express the conflicting character of much of human experience, the twin facets every sensation holds and which it is the poet's particular task to represent.

Neither the scope nor the structure of metaphor has altered much since classical times, and its basic definition remains the same. Metaphor may be most simply described as a means of viewing one thing in terms of another. It is made up of two parts, the tenor, that which we are talking about, and the vehicle, the term through which we are portraying it.[1] The Greek vocabulary is rich in metaphorical terms; *kleis*, key, was also used figuratively in the sense of the collar bone on account of the fancied similarity in shape between the two. The common ground between two elements may be their appearance, or the feeling and sensation they provoke. Metaphor works not only through replacement of one term, but through the transferred attribute; we speak of a bitter disappointment because its effect on us is like that of a bitter taste. At the root of metaphoric thinking lie notions of comparison and contrast;[2] the speaker likens or contrasts the phenomena he wishes to describe to what is familiar and available in his language. The Homeric simile provides a clear example of this device at work when the poet selects his vehicles from objects which lie within his audience's experience in order to convey the heightened nature of the heroic world in which his characters move, where every thought and deed surpasses the everyday. Mass emotion, psychological turmoil and complex human relationships all become vivid and intelligible through comparison and contrast with familiar feeling.[3] Polarity and analogy are devices of measurement as well as description: the metaphor works by degree, attributing to one thing more or less of a quality than to another. Sappho represents herself as paler than grass when she perceives the man sitting next to the friend she loves (31.14). Metaphor serves as a tool for demonstration which can impose an external order on a set of apparently random elements, arranging them into meaningful sequence. The task of theories of metaphor is to examine the terms which the metaphor involves, and to explore the different

[1] The terms 'tenor' and 'vehicle' were first coined by I.A. Richards in *The Philosophy of Rhetoric* (Oxford, 1936/1979), p.96.

[2] On comparison and contrast as early tools in Greek philosophical and scientific thinking see G.E.R. Lloyd, *Polarity and Analogy* (Cambridge, 1966).

[3] A brief discussion of the uses Homer makes of the simile may be found in M. Coffey, 'The function of the Homeric simile', *AJPh* 78 (1957), pp.113-32. For a more extensive treatment see H. Fränkel, *Die homerischen Gleichnisse* (Göttingen, 1921).

relations it establishes between them. It is a task which raises more fundamental questions concerning the nature of the linguistic medium, the link between name and object, word and idea. The convention of language promotes the illusion that we may readily identify objects 'out there' and refer to them by the proper use of their name. This is the assumption on which most ancient commentators work, taking as their starting point the notion of a language governed by nature, in which a word signifies an object through a natural suitability of word to thing. Plato's *Cratylus* explores this idea: the principal test of a name's correctness, the dialogue proposes, is its capacity to convey and teach the essence of the thing to which it is attached. According to Cratylus, if X is not the correct name of a given object, in keeping with these standards, it makes no difference if everyone calls it so. The correct name must satisfy two further conditions; it should be capable of etymological resolution into other names whose combination is also appropriate to the thing it describes, and must, in some sense, be a verbal representation of the object itself. The argument breaks down when the speakers attempt to demonstrate the point by the term *sklêrotês*, hardness, whose harsh consonants are supposed to convey the very essence of the word. When Socrates seeks further to reduce linguistic compounds into linguistic simples, and to provide a *logos*, or logical account, for the elements he has obtained, he is led to conclude that language is governed by convention and norm alone.[4] Despite his proofs, theories of natural language persisted side by side with the 'conventionalist' account and continued to lend credence to the notion that speech operated *kata phusin*, according to nature.[5] Modern theorists have entirely rejected the exclusive relation between word and object, and make of language a tri-partite structure involving subject, object and the

---

[4] Theories of natural language, and the discussion in the *Cratylus* are explored in M. Schofield, 'The dénouement of the *Cratylus*', and B. Williams, 'Cratylus' theory of names and its refutation', in M. Schofield and M. Nussbaum (eds), *Language and Logos* (Cambridge, 1982), pp.61-81 and 83-93.

[5] Aristotle presupposes the notion of language operating according to nature or norm when he states, at *Rh.*1404bf.: 'We all use metaphors in our ordinary discourse.' For further treatment of the notion see D.A. Russell, *'Longinus': On the Sublime* (Oxford, 1964), p.127.

linguistic medium itself which interacts with the other two.[6] Saussure's linguistic theory describes language as an arbitrary system of signs where no implicit bond exists between a name and the object it represents. The word, or sign, is the union of a signifier and a signified, of the denotative and connotative facets of a term which stand in random relation to one another.[7] According to this view, a table has no more of tableness in it than if we were to call it chair.

The nature of the connection between a name and an object raises questions concerning meaning itself, and its expression through the linguistic code. To return to Cratylus' argument, if a tight bond exists between a word and thing, each word may rightly describe only one thing. Its *phusis* is something fixed and immutable, dictated either by nature or by norm. Norm comes into play to explain the capacity of words to change their meaning over time, a feature recognised though not fully accounted for by ancient theorists. Modern scholarship rejects notions of fixed meaning, whether over time or at any given point, and has sought to explain how a single word may possess a multiplicity of meanings.[8] Saussure denies the idea of nomenclature, whereby a series of names is attached to a set of fixed ideas. He places arbitrariness within the heart of the concept as well as in the code designed to refer to it. The random and differential nature of the sign finds its echo in the shifting body of phenomena which it describes, and has many applications according to how we divide up the world and how we perceive one sign in relation to those surrounding it. The body of concepts to which we assign names is like a rainbow, a spectrum whose shades merge into one another and on which we impose artificial colour distinctions. Because experience is a continuum, capable of sustaining infinite methods of division, meaning is as flexible as signs themselves, shaped by individual and collective

---

[6] P. Wheelwright, *Metaphor and Reality* (Bloomington, 1962), p.26f.

[7] Saussure's theory has been published as the *Cours de linguistique générale* (5th ed. Paris, 1955); now translated and annotated by Roy Harris (London, 1983). For a useful presentation of his ideas see J. Culler, *Saussure* (Glasgow, 1976).

[8] 'The meaning of a word – in actual speech – is identical with those elements of the user's (speaker's or hearer's) subjective apprehension of the referent denoted by the word which he apprehends as expressed by it.' G. Stern, *Meaning and Change of Meaning* (Gothenburg, 1931), p.45.

perceptions and beliefs.

These two different approaches to language erect very different points of departure for accounts of metaphor, an important element within the linguistic medium. Where one word has one meaning, and meaning itself is absolute, metaphor can be no more than a departure from the nature or norm the term possesses. It represents an attempt to confuse the fixed boundaries that language sets up between different categories of sense. Implicit in Aristotle's choice of the term *metaphora* is the notion of displacement, of the transposition of a word from its rightful place to an alien one. Indeed, a metaphor is doubly foreign to its position, a name that belongs elsewhere and which dislocates the proper word.[9] Cicero's description shares in Aristotle's bias when he speaks of metaphor as a kind of borrowing: 'You take from elsewhere what you have not got at hand' (*de oratore* 3.15b). Metaphor, when viewed as transfer, does not disturb the notion of natural or conventional usage since the figure does no more than to supplant or supplement an adequate literal term. Modern linguistics takes an opposite approach, moving not from norm to metaphor, but from metaphor to ordinary speech; since language stands as something quite independent from the external reality we assume it to convey, metaphor is merely an extreme example of the process every speech act describes. The very fact of referring involves symbolic representation, talking of one thing in terms of another, of an object or idea through the vehicle language provides.[10] Representation is not a natural relationship, not pure imitation, but, like Aristotelian mimesis, alters the very fabric of the thing which it portrays.[11] This explains how new meaning may arise through the use of existing vocabulary for, as Shelley writes:

> Language is vitally metaphorical. It marks the before unapprehended relations of things, and perpetuates their

---

[9] P. Ricoeur, *The Rule of Metaphor* (London, 1978), p.17.

[10] A number of modern critics have argued for the inherently metaphoric nature of language. See in particular Richards, op.cit., and Wheelwright, *The Burning Fountain* (Bloomington, 1954) and *Metaphor*, op.cit.

[11] Ricoeur suggests this way of understanding the concept of mimesis, presenting it not as pure imitation but as a combination of 'human reality' with 'an original creation'. Ricoeur, op.cit., p.37f.

apprehensions, until words, which represent them, become,
through time, signs for portions or classes of thought.[12]

Within this reorientation, metaphor appears not as a deviation
from the norm, transgressing the dictates of syntax and sense,
but a paradigm for all language functions.

Modern theory does not entirely remove the role of convention,
recognising that words do possess a sense which the majority
agrees upon. It replaces the division between a proper and a
derived meaning with the distinction between signification, in
which a signifier means a signified, and symbolisation, in which
a first symbolised signifies a second.[13] The first process assumes
exact representation while the second openly acknowledges the
symbolic nature of speech. Again Plato anticipates modern
advances in his perception that words may 'mean' in different
fashions. In the *Sophist* he separates naming, the function of the
single term, from stating, something that can only be done by a
complex linguistic item.[14] Aristotle marked no such distinction
between the individual word and the phrase when he defined the
metaphor. It is, according to his formulation, merely one item in
a long list of possible noun types including 'standard terms,
dialect terms, decorative terms, neologisms, lengthened words,
shortened words and altered words' (*Poetics* 1457b). His
definition of metaphor itself is firmly rooted in the individual
noun, strictly terminological in its account of how the figure
operates. It involves 'the transferred use of a term that properly
belongs to something else. The transference can be from genus to
species, from species to genus, from species to species, or
analogical' (*Poetics* 1457b). His failure to distinguish between
the single word and the broader unit of meaning encourages the
confusion between figure and trope, which are both included in
his account. While the figure does indeed rearrange words at the
level of the whole phrase, a trope is merely a change or deviation
affecting the meaning of the individual term. Modern linguistics
attributes a double character to the word. Speech, according to

---

[12] Quoted in Richards, op.cit., p.90.

[13] The notion of secondary signification builds on Frege's fundamental
distinction between sense and reference. See G. Frege, 'On sense and reference',
in *Philosophical Writings of Gottlob Frege*, trans. Max Black and Peter Geech
(Oxford, 1952).

[14] Cf. Julia Annas, 'Knowledge and language: the *Theaetetus* and the
Cratylus', in Schofield and Nussbaum, op.cit., pp.95-114.

Benveniste, contains two elements, language or signs, and discourse or sentences.[15] The word exists as a discrete member of the lexical code, a dictionary listing, and as part of the broader unit, the sentence. This division permits a closer appreciation of the effect of metaphor on language, including the change at the level of the word, which Aristotle describes, and the alteration of the phrase as a whole. Metaphor may entirely recast the sense of an expression without seeming to disturb its grammatical construction. Thus a storm in a tea cup is a very different thing from a storm over the Western Isles. In the first phrase the individual word remains the 'focus' of the metaphor, but exists in relation to its surrounding terms or 'frame'.[16] Metaphor acts not only on language in its identifying function, but also on the qualities, classes and relations it predicates.

The ancient view of metaphor, by emphasising the substitution of one isolated term for another, makes of the figure a kind of puzzle, a riddle or hunt for a single unwritten term which the metaphor has displaced. This was the approach frequently taken by the scholiasts as they sought to unpack metaphor, to identify its component parts and the common ground between them. They looked for its diagrammatic qualities, the exact matching of the attributes of the misplaced word to the new one, and rhetorical and poetic practice sometimes satisfied their demands. The familiar metaphor of the ship of state rests on the fact that both ship and city possess their helmsman or leader, their crew or citizen body. Aristotle demonstrates the analogical transfer metaphor may involve with his exact analysis of the expressions 'Dionysus' shield' and 'Ares' cup' (*Poetics* 1457b). A similarity between the new expression and the old was the mark of a successful metaphor which served as little more than a condensed simile. Aristotle joins the two figures when he writes: 'The simile is also metaphor' (*Rhetoric* 3.1406b), and Demetrius follows his account when he cautions: 'If a metaphor seems risky, turn it into a simile ... A simile is an extended metaphor' (*On Style* 80).[17] Without a perceptible likeness between its parts, a

---

[15] E. Benveniste, *Problèmes de linguistique générale* (Paris, 1966).

[16] The focus/frame paradigm first appears in M. Black, *Models and Metaphors* (Ithaca, 1962).

[17] For a comprehensive treatment of ancient views on simile and metaphor, and the changing primacy of place they observed, see M. McCall, *Ancient Rhetorical Theories of Simile and Comparison* (Cambridge, Mass., 1969).

metaphor will fail, and Cicero places the pleasure we derive from metaphor in our apprehension of the underlying similarity between its parts (*de oratore* 3.160-3). The modern theories developed by I.A. Richards, Black and others view metaphor not as a jigsaw that lacks a single piece, but as a composite which involves two elements, both simultaneously present in the phrase. Within one symbol, it holds two thoughts of different things, two different missing parts of the different context of its entire meaning. Metaphor emerges as no mere verbal matter, not 'a shifting and displacement of words, but a borrowing between and intercourse of thoughts, a transaction between contexts'.[18] Many different elements can be brought into play, and many different kinds of relations exist between them. Metaphor does not bring together only noun and noun, but word and idea, and may involve similarity, antithesis and the juxtaposition of its parts. Similarity is no longer seen as the key to metaphor, but, indeed, Ricoeur argues that the metaphor creates the similarity rather than giving some pre-existent likeness verbal form.[19] Both likeness and unlikeness may enter into a single metaphor which opens with the one and moves over to the other. Shakespeare writes of Antony: 'For his bounty/ There was no winter in't. An autumn 'twas/ That grew the more by reaping' (*Antony and Cleopatra* V.ii.86-8). Here he draws on the traditional associations of autumn, its abundance and fruitfulness, proceeding through relations of similarity. However, Antony is unlike autumn in one critical respect, his bounty will not peak and decline.[20] Such 'relevant unlikeness'[21] is an effective device in both ancient and modern metaphors. When Clytemnestra describes the delight she feels at the rush of Agamemnon's blood, rejoicing 'no less than the crop rejoices/ In the Zeus-given moisture at the birth of the bud' (*Agamemnon*, 1391-2), the impact of the expression lies in the tragic gap between blood, symbolising sterility and death, and rain which evokes fertility and regeneration of life. One critic, following Aristotle's original terms, has distinguished two possible metaphoric processes, one 'epiphoric', the other 'diaphoric'. 'Epiphor' builds upon a

---

[18] Richards, op.cit., p.94.
[19] Ricoeur, op.cit., p.86.
[20] This example is quoted in W. Nowottny, *The Language Poets Use* (London, 1962, 1981), p.64.
[21] M. Silk, *Interaction in Poetic Imagery* (Cambridge, 1974), p.5.

previous likeness, while 'diaphor' creates new patterns of meaning through antithesis and synthesis. W.H. Auden's *Fall of Rome* shows both at work; until the last stanza, the poem proceeds largely through epiphor, addressing the present state of civilisation through the symbol of Rome. In the final stanza, however, the poet turns to diaphor in the simple contrast that concludes the work:

> Altogether elsewhere, vast
> Herds of reindeer move across
> Miles and miles of golden moss,
> Silently and very fast.
>   (*Nones*, pp.32-3)[22]

Metaphor may exist independently of a likeness or difference between its parts and relies rather on the variety of qualities contained within whatever it fixes on. André Breton gives the widest possible scope to the device when he writes, 'To compare two objects as remote from one another as possible, or by any other method to bring them together in sudden and striking fashion, this remains the highest task to which poetry can aspire.'[23] The poet's capacity to create a significant partnership between different elements, often belonging to widely divergent categories of sense, is virtually boundless, resting upon the endless connotative possibilities a word possesses. In appealing not only to logical relations, but to intuition and feeling, metaphor breaks down the divisions everyday speech erects between thought and sensation. While the ancient critics saw metaphor as speaking of X in terms of Y, the moderns view it as feeling, thinking and perceiving X in terms proper to Y, terms which may draw on the associative and suggestive aura of the expression involved. Those very attributes which may appear 'nonsensical' can convey meaning within their novel context.

Ancient and modern theories of metaphor now stand distinct; the first is grounded in the notion of comparison or substitution, where one term is replaced by another by virtue of some recognisable likeness between the two. The second defines metaphor as interaction, the co-presence of both tenor and vehicle in one expression whose meaning is a result of their

---

[22] Quoted by Wheelwright, *Metaphor*, op.cit., p.87.
[23] Richards, op.cit., p.123.

interchange.[24] The essence of the figure is that it may not be defined either as one element or the other, neither the 'real' or prose meaning, nor the figurative way of expressing it. Its effectiveness depends on a certain tension between its parts; too great a likeness would destroy the impact of the metaphor, where neither element must overwhelm the other. When, in *Richard II*, Shakespeare describes the king in terms of the sun, the sun does not become Richard nor Richard the sun. What does occur is that the sovereign's relation to his kingdom takes on all the significance of the sun's role in the lives of men and nature, and his fall assumes cosmic proportions, disturbing the harmony of the entire universe. The concept of interaction, a vivid sense of two-in-one, permits the necessary distinction between live and dead metaphor to become clear, between the catachresis that occurs in everyday speech, and new word use in poetic discourse.[25] It was the nineteenth-century critic Fontanier who first asserted that the mark of a true metaphor is that its use is free, and not imposed by some gap in the existing vocabulary.[26] Unlike catachresis, which develops such terms as 'family tree' or the 'boot of a car', metaphor retains its original emotive impact. Ordinary speech rapidly assimilates new word use, confining expressions to a limited range of meaning in order that all men may mean the same thing, but poetic speech builds on the multiple levels of sense a single term contains. While ancient commentators acknowledged the two types of discourse, they failed to carry the distinction any further, and rarely examined the particular role of the second within the literary work. Metaphor was necessity first, and verbal embellishment afterwards. The substitution theory may explain metaphor which arises in the case of necessity, where the impact of the figure is restricted to the individual term within the lexical code, but interaction alone can account for the innovative, evocative language of the poet, fluid and polysemous in nature.[27]

[24] The interaction theory of metaphor is outlined in M. Black, 'More about metaphor' in A. Ortony (ed.), *Metaphor and Thought* (Cambridge, 1979), pp.19-34; and J. Martin and R. Harré, 'Metaphor in science', in D.S. Miall (ed.), *Metaphor: Problems and Perspectives* (Brighton, 1982), pp.89-105.

[25] The question of ancient awareness of dead metaphor and of catachresis is discussed in Silk, op.cit., pp.27f. and 210f.

[26] P. Fontanier, *Les Figures du discours* (1830) (Paris, 1968), p.213f.

[27] Ricoeur denies any necessary contradiction between the two theories, arguing that they belong to different kinds of speech acts: 'Accordingly, there is

The theory of interaction allows us to come closer to the actual dynamics of the metaphor and the interplay between the literal and figurative levels of meaning which it inevitably involves. It is a cardinal feature of metaphor that within the expression some terms refer literally to one situation and figuratively to a second, while others have only a literal sense, and belong to the second situation alone.[28] Blake's poem *A Poison Tree* illustrates the co-presence of these two elements, and the poet's rapid passage between the two levels of thought:

> I was angry with my friend:
> I told my wrath, my wrath did end.
> I was angry with my foe:
> I told it not, my wrath did grow.
>
> And I waterd it in fears,
> Night and morning with my tears:
> And I sunned it with smiles,
> And with soft deceitful wiles.
>
> And it grew both day and night,
> Till it bore an apple bright.
> And my foe beheld it shine
> And he knew that it was mine.
>
> And into my garden stole,
> When the night had veild the pole;
> In the morning glad I see,
> My foe outstretched beneath the tree.

The apple stands both as an actual fruit, growing upon a literal tree, and as the symbol for the repressed anger of the speaker, developing within his mind where it responds to attention and care. The two levels of meaning coincide most forcibly when the literal and figurative apples combine to destroy their victim.

---

no conflict properly speaking between the theory of substitution (or of deviation) and the interaction theory. The latter describes the dynamics of the metaphorical statement; it alone deserves to be called a semantic theory of metaphor. The substitution theory denotes the impact of this dynamic on the lexical code where it sees a deviation; in doing so, it offers the semiotic equivalent of the semantic process.' Ricoeur, op.cit., p.157. For a discussion of the shortcomings of both theories as comprehensive accounts of metaphor see J.R. Searle, 'Metaphor', in Ortony, op.cit., pp.92-123.

[28] Cf. P. Henle, *Language, Thought and Culture* (Ann Arbor, 1958), p.181.

In this interaction between tenor and vehicle, the poet selects only some attributes of his term for verbal figuration. Others are best left in the literal realm, since they might otherwise deflect from the target of the metaphor. If when a writer spoke of the roses of a woman's cheek, we thought of thorns and green leaves in addition to the flower's softness and delicate shading, the purpose of the image would be lost. Some symbols command instant recognition of their essential qualities, but other, less familiar ones, require careful poetic handling. Modern theory has come up with the concept of abstraction to explain how, in metaphor, the poet shapes the meaning of the words he uses and the concepts and associations they call into play.[29] He abstracts the meaning required, making the word lose its reference to a particular object and take on a generalised value applicable to many different contexts. Thus, in *King Lear*, clothing appears in a variety of settings where it announces the themes of need, display, concealment and the adornment of majesty. Different poets may abstract different qualities from the words that they choose for symbolic status, in accordance with the themes they wish to highlight. The bird in Pindar is notable not for its power of song, the property evoked in other lyric poets' mention of the creature, but for its flight. Abstraction reveals the flexible nature of language, and further undermines the ancient portrait of metaphor as the exact matching of the attributes of one thing to those of another.

In addition to examining its function and structure, ancient and modern theorists have approached metaphor from the standpoint of its application, where its usage is most in evidence, and what this reveals of its character. Attempts have been made to classify metaphor according to the tenors and vehicles it contains, and the kind of interchange they promote. In this area, views of metaphor have remained fairly constant, and Aristotle's distinctions still hold firm. He defined transfers between the animate and inanimate realms, which may travel in either direction. Anthropomorphic metaphors refer to inanimate objects in terms belonging to the human body and its parts, common in the most diverse languages and literary forms.[30] We

---

[29] Abstraction is defined in H. Konrad, *Etude sur la métaphore* (Vrin, 1959), p.88f.

[30] S. Ullmann, *Semantics: An Introduction to the Science of Meaning* (Oxford, 1962, 1983), p.214f.

thus may speak of the brow of a hill, the foot of a bed, the heart of the matter. The animal kingdom is another major source of metaphor, generating such familiar expressions as crane, the cock of a gun, the muscle which the Romans derived from *musculus*, or little mouse. A human being may be likened to an inexhaustible variety of animals, as Semonides' extensive catalogue of women illustrates. In English, people can be catty, mulish or sheepish, they may ape or lionise. The transfer from the inanimate to the animate realm attributes life to emotion and to thought, representing abstract ideas in concrete, tangible terms in accordance with the notion of the life-force they appear to possess. Words in Greek are winged, flying from the speaker's mouth to the listener. Light and its various manifestations stand as a frequent symbol for joy, safety and deliverance, while in English abstractions may illuminate, highlight and dazzle. A final common class of metaphor involves synaesthesia, the transfer of perception from one sense to another. Cicero already identified this as one of the particular qualities of metaphor when he evoked such phrases as a 'whiff of urbanity' and the 'sweetness of speech' (*de oratore* 3.161). Aeschylus speaks of the trumpet which sets the shore ablaze with sound (*Persae* 395), and long before Baudelaire set out his theory of verbal synaesthesia in the poem *Correspondences*, Shakespeare described a strain of music as 'a sweet sound / That breathes upon a bank of violets / Stealing and giving odour' (*Twelfth Night*, I.i.5-7). Modern theorists have examined language for areas of dense metaphoric speech. The term 'centres of expansion' describes those categories which provide the vehicles of the metaphor, 'centres of attraction' those which contain the tenors or the subjects which require expression through the vocabulary metaphor can supply.[31] Subjects of particular concern to a community or individual author will draw synonyms from many directions, many metaphorical in character. A perennial centre of attraction is the theme of death, an area which men hesitate to approach by direct means. Metaphors may be studied as a key to collective values, fears and ambitions, indicating areas both of immediate importance, and those of such remoteness that metaphor alone can express their unknown quality. The similes and metaphors selected by the

---

[31] Ibid., pp.149-50, 201-4.

individual author likewise direct the reader towards his dominant interests as he seeks to vary their presentation by introducing terms from different domains. Battle and strife in Homer, athletic victory in Pindar, both serve simultaneously as centres of expansion and attraction.

The functions that metaphor fills are as varied as the realms which generate and attract it. Ancient critics took a somewhat restricted view of its role, perceiving it either as a means of papering over the gaps in the existing vocabulary, or as a mere stylistic device, one in a long line of possible ornamental tropes and figures of speech. Metaphor is most frequently considered as belonging to the art of rhetoric; here it plays a considerable part in lending clarity, warmth, facility, appropriateness and, above all, elegance or urbanity to the speaker's words. These are Aristotelian terms, and appear within the philosopher's discussion of how the orator may best achieve his aim, that of effective persuasion.[32] The instructive value of the metaphor, and all rhetorical ornamentation must finally be didactic in its end, lies in the pleasure of understanding which follows on the initial shock the figure provokes. Our delight in apprehending its sense makes us more willing to accept the truth of the speaker's words (*Rhetoric* 3.1410b).

Grandeur, majesty and pithiness continue to appear in ancient accounts of the contribution of metaphor,[33] but no commentator focuses on its power to innovate, to say something new. Metaphor remains, in essence, an unusual way of naming things. The modern approach is radically different; it regards metaphor as a means of apprehending and portraying ideas which escape direct representation. It is a device of symbolisation which achieves its fullest scope not within rhetoric, but in the poet's speech. Here it vastly increases the vocabulary at his reach, and enables him to introduce terms from diverse realms of experience to bear on the situation or emotion he wishes to describe. Metaphor can alone achieve the exact shade of meaning the poet aims at. Most important, metaphor permits the poet to employ language at both the literal and figurative levels of meaning, and

---

[32] Cf. discussion of Aristotle's view of rhetoric in G. Kennedy, *Classical Rhetoric* (London, 1980).

[33] Kennedy, op.cit. and W.B. Stanford, *Greek Metaphor: Studies in Theory and Practice* (Oxford, 1936), ch.3.

promotes the traffic between what enters the work as part of the 'real' situation the writer treats and that which comes in as extra-verbal figuration in accordance with the broader themes and significance he wishes to explore.[34] In *The Man with the Blue Guitar*, Wallace Stevens demonstrates how, through metaphor, a work may deal simultaneously with the phenomenal world and the world of values:

> The man bent over his guitar,
> A shearsman of sorts. The day was green.
>
> They said, 'You have a blue guitar,
> You do not play things as they are.'
>
> The man replied, 'Things as they are
> Are changed upon the blue guitar.'
>
> And they said then, 'But play, you must,
> A tune beyond us, yet ourselves,
>
> A tune upon the blue guitar,
> Of things exactly as they are.'

> (*Collected Poems*, p.165)

Metaphor's capacity to describe areas of heightened experience is of particular importance to the poet: it is his task to give expression to emotion and intuition in novel ways, setting the stamp of his own perceptions on feelings that all may recognise, but few understand. The symbol of the Grecian Urn in Keats' Ode permits the poet to suggest the seemingly antithetical notions of transience and fixity, fleeting beauty and permanent representation, the twin faces of the single work. Modern critics have also looked at metaphor within the broader structure of the literary work where it unifies different portions through recurrent motifs, which gain in significance with repeated evocation.[35] The movement and development of a metaphor can accompany the progress of the action, and in Sophocles' *Oedipus Rex*, the king's metaphoric blindness resolves itself in the tragic scene where he appears having put out his own eyes. Whatever its specific role or

---

[34] Nowottny, op.cit., p.85.

[35] For an excellent treatment of one author's development of metaphoric motifs see A. Lebeck, *The Oresteia: A Study in Language and Structure* (Washington D.C., 1971).

application, metaphor invariably has a profound effect on the language of the literary text, capturing the essence of the poetic discourse. While in ordinary speech the arbitrary, conventional nature of the sign divides meaning from sensation, metaphor in poetry allows sense and feeling to co-exist within a single term. The sign is understood as symbol in its multiplicity of facets and associations. The individual term ceases to be a means towards the end of external reality, or towards the orator's truth, and becomes significant in itself. When language is made up of words possessing their own depth and density of meaning, the experiences it relates become vivid and immediate, invested with the quality of *energeia*, actuality, which Aristotle discerned in the poet's speech (*Rhetoric* 3.1412a).

Two major distinctions characterise the different accounts of metaphor ancient and modern theorists have devised. One concerns their view of language itself, the other the rhetorical or poetic orientation of an age. The changing perception of metaphor from classical to modern times may, in part, be seen as keeping pace with the shift in emphasis away from rhetoric towards the 'literary', from rhetorical analysis to literary criticism. The two arts possess their own distinctive aims and requirements; rhetoric was designed to persuade, poetry to purge the emotions of pity and of fear. Originally quite discrete, the division between the two realms grew blurred when the sophists and thinkers of the fifth century B.C. became concerned with achieving a poetic style in prose, and the figures and tropes, the rare and ornamental words which the poet devised were appropriated by the orator. The functions of the two arts were confused; Plato speaks of the manner in which the rhapsode produces fear and sorrow (*Ion* 535c-d), and Socrates asserts that if one were to take from poetry its rhythm and its metre, only the words which served the orator's end would remain (502c).[36] The assimilation of rhetoric to poetics profoundly altered men's perception of the second of the two, and from the time of Gorgias the practical techniques of speaking were thought to give guidance in the evaluation of poetry. Rhetoric was conceptualised from the very first, lending itself readily to classification

---

[36] Cf. J. de Romilly, *Magic and Rhetoric in Ancient Greece* (Cambridge, Mass. and London, 1975), ch.1 on Gorgias' account of rhetoric and poetry.

in terms of its figures of thought and speech.[37] Poetry resisted such parcelling out, so long as commentators hesitated to categorise what still lay in the undefined realm of inspiration. When the critics of antiquity wanted to examine literature, they naturally borrowed the rhetorical system ready at hand, and metaphor was viewed from its perspective. The actual conditions of literary discourse in part determined the rhetorical stance. When a poem was primarily a spoken thing, available in written form only to the very few, it demanded to be treated as speech, linear in character, limited to a single recitation. An audience would have little opportunity to seize its finer points of imagery or structure, and criticism addressed the impression that the listener, not the reader would receive. The modern close analysis and *explication de texte* are made possible only by our ready access to the written work which bears repeated reading and examination, comparison with similar texts. While modern criticism discusses the designs of the author, the expectations of the reader, writer and critic all, an ancient commentator would rather look at the immediate impact of the poem on its audience. It is perhaps our transformation from an audience of listeners to one of solitary readers that has opened up the way for a closer appreciation of that most literary of devices, the metaphor.

---

[37] The notion of the borrowing of the rhetorical system for literary criticism among early commentators is raised in Kennedy, op.cit., p. 108f. and in his *The Art of Persuasion in Greece* (London 1963), ch.1.

2
Pindaric Metaphor, Function and Form

Pindaric verse illustrates the many features of metaphor that ancient and modern theorists have discerned in the device. Metaphor gives to his poetry its quality of vividness, motion and immediacy, making the language dense and compressed. Each individual word possesses multiple associations, and suggestion and deliberate conflation of meaning all account for the opaque quality of the verse where every expression is significant both in itself and as part of its broader context. Without metaphor, Pindar's poetry would lose its unique character in terms of its language, structure and themes, and a large degree of the impression of unity the ode conveys would disappear. Metaphor has a more specific function within the verse than the mere vivifying of poetic discourse; its role in Pindar addresses the particular character of the genre, interacting with and promoting the elements the poem must contain, and the structuring devices that hold together the individual song. An initial approach to metaphor in Pindar must explore the particular suitability of the figure for its place within the design and contents of his epinician verse.

Metaphor contributes to the overall aim of the victory song where praise of the subject and his triumph must act as the guiding principle.[1] Direct eulogy of the poem's patron would quickly dull, and the epinician genre contains many elements which promote more indirectly the end of praise. Pindar turns to metaphoric expression and ways of thought as a means of

---

[1] Cf. E.L. Bundy, *Studia Pindarica* I, II, *University of California Publications in Classical Philology* 18 (1962), pp.1-34 and 39-52 for an account of epinicia as pure encomium.

varying the language at his disposal, and of introducing new realms of vocabulary and themes. In presenting the laudandus, he does not proceed through direct, but through symbolic representation, not just celebrating the success that is the subject of his song, but evaluating it and setting it against a broader backdrop. He sees victory both in terms of what it is, and of what it is not, comparing and contrasting it with like and unlike. He evokes both positive and negative terms of reference, introducing diverse characters and events as varied perspectives on the matter at hand. The individual metaphor, its structure and sense, may be seen as a paradigm for the broader fashion in which Pindar approaches his subject; the metaphor brings together two different elements into one whole, using one as a perspective on the other. Thus the poet mingles victory with other spheres, viewing it through the various lenses they provide. Metaphor discovers patterns of relations between its component parts just as the poet reveals connections of likeness and difference between the victor and the external world. In mixing different categories of words and meanings, the metaphor demands that we look beneath the surface sense a phrase may have towards its underlying significance. This process describes Pindar's treatment of his patron and the patron's triumph as the poet perceives within the immediate deed the abiding meanings that may be drawn from achievement and its celebration in song. The central place that metaphor holds within Pindar's verse rests on its power to perform at the local level the transformations that the poet works on his subject as a whole.

A close examination of the way in which Pindaric metaphor operates reveals the devices the poet uses to direct his audience to the larger concerns of his verse. Metaphor promotes non-literal understanding in one of two ways; a statement may appear non-sensical at an initial reading, and force us to look again for a figurative sense. When Pindar declares at *P.* 2.80 that he is *abaptistos*, unsinkable, the term can only be taken in its metaphoric vein. Metaphoric language can also signal its presence in expressions which seem out of context, and which make no immediate sense in terms of the surrounding elements. Examining what came before, or what follows on afterwards, we re-appraise the meaning of the statement and replace its face value with a non-literal one. Water, Pindar declares in the first line of *O.* 1, is the best of substances, but its relevance to the

Olympic Games, which the poet goes on to evoke, only becomes clear when we focus not on the substance itself, but on the notions of excellence and pre-eminence which unify the opening portions of the ode. Pindaric metaphor clearly demonstrates how the figure of speech involves an attribution that is either immediately self-contradictory, or obviously false within the context, and so makes us search for a secondary level of sense.[2] Figuration is the hallmark of metaphor, and of the Pindaric ode where representation replaces the direct account.

Each individual metaphor involves patterns of relations between its parts, presenting in miniature the different kinds of connections which can exist between the laudandus and the external characters and events the poet introduces. The analogy the metaphor describes may be one of likeness or of difference; a city is like a ship in terms of its organisation, with the leader at the helm (*P.* 1.86), while a poem is unlike the sculpture which must remain permanently fixed on its pedestal (*N.* 5.1f.). Metaphor builds either on functional relationships, comparing and contrasting what two things do, or through emotive appeal, when the poet draws on two similar or antithetical realms of feeling. Poetry is like a drug because it causes men to forget their pain (*P.* 3.64f.; *N.* 4.1-5), and the victory comparable to marriage in the joyous sensations both arouse (*O.* 7.1f.). Such connections between Pindar's tenors and vehicles may be perceived as devices either of association or identification; an object is called by the name of something linked or associated with it, as when Pindar uses metonymy in substituting the wreath for victory or the Muse for song.[3] Identification involves both imitation and symbolism; Pindar presents the poet as an athlete whose task demands that he undergo the same risks and display the same skills as the man he celebrates. Many metaphors call simultaneously on relations of function and of feeling, of association and symbolism. The cup functions like the song, filled with the inebriating power of song as wine, and is also an integral part of the celebration of victory and the communal

---

[2] M.C. Beardsley, *Aesthetics* (New York, 1958, repr. Indianapolis, Cambridge, 1981), p.140f.
[3] On the links between the tropological and the metaphoric figure, and their relation to the general processes of language itself, see R. Jakobson, 'Two aspects of language and two types of aphasic disturbances', in R. Jakobson and M. Hallé, *The Fundamentals of Language* (The Hague, 1956).

feeling associated with the feast (*N.* 9.48f.). In describing one situation by means of another, metaphor carries the sensations attached to the symbol into the heart of the situation symbolised, collapsing boundaries between meaning and feeling, and establishing patterns of relations in the affective as well as the cognitive spheres.[4] At the broader level of the poem, Pindar brings to victory the aura of the events with which it is compared, and permits the triumph itself to diffuse its own symbols and associations into neighbouring areas.

The objects, people and events which Pindar draws into his network of metaphor are as varied as the links which exist between the terms of his figures, and relate directly to the contents of the ode as well as to its particular structure of sense. He seeks the broadest possible stage for his presentation of his subject, building on established patterns of relations in order to uncover new ones. His analogies join objects with ideas, people with abstract notions, the animate with the inanimate, and ignore the semantic categories that non-poetic language observes. He gives the abstract tangible form when he presents mortal fortunes in the shape of winds and waves which veer from side to side (*P.* 3.104-6). Animate mixes with animate in his portrayals of the athlete and poet as eagles (*N.* 3.80f.), inanimate with animate when virtue becomes a plant that grows (*N.* 8.40). It is a feature of Pindaric metaphor that at least one of the two terms must belong to the concrete realm, for two abstracts alone fail to generate the visual or sensual quality that is so important a part of symbolic representation.[5] The diverse elements that metaphor can include permit Pindar to introduce the essential material that the ode must contain. The epinician genre demands that the poet mention the critical factors of the event he celebrates. He must refer to the name of the victor, his father and city, the Games where he competed and the particular contest in which he achieved his triumph. Pindar's passage between the actual and the figurative spheres is frequently virtually imperceptible as a single term forms the pivot or link between the literal and the metaphoric parts of the

---

[4] Cf. Henle, op.cit. for 'induced content' of metaphor, p.191.

[5] S. Ullmann, *Language and Style* (Oxford, 1964) gives examples of how metaphor fails when it attempts to bring together two abstracts; see p.176.

phrase.[6] When, at *O.* 6.22f. the poet writes:

ὦ Φίντις, ἀλλὰ ζεῦξον ἤ-
δη μοι σθένος ἡμιόνων,
ᾇ τάχος, ὄφ'ρα κελεύθῳ τ᾽ ἐν καθαρᾷ
βάσομεν ὄκχον, ἵκωμαί τε π'ρὸς ἀνδρῶν
καὶ γένος·

Phintis, yoke up for me the strength of mules with all speed,
so that we may set the chariot on the clear road and I may
reach the theme of their origin.

only the description of the 'pure' character of the road points us
away from the actual mule race towards poetic figuration. Pindar
also draws on events in the laudandus' life, on the past history of
his family and city, on current affairs which may lend further
substance to his praise and address areas of collective concern.
Although part of a particular genre, the individual ode cannot be
seen as wholly divorced from the social and historical
environment of its day, and references to actual events are
embedded even in the most figurative expressions the poet
devises.[7] Through verbal figuration, Pindar passes between the
real and the 'literary', allowing the weight of the former to lend
credence to the latter, and the terms of the latter to aggrandise
the former. *Nemean* 3, 4, 5 and 6, each composed to celebrate a
citizen of sea-faring Aegina, display a marked amount of
maritime imagery in keeping with the character of the island,
and *N.* 5 opens with an image of sculpting, the art in which its
citizens excelled. Even the rocky topography of Delphi finds a
place within the extended metaphor that opens *P.* 6 where the
poet describes his poem as a strong edifice which the
stone-carrying winds cannot disturb (12-14).

Metaphor carries the shift between the information the poet
must include, or considers relevant to the matter at hand, and
the broader message he wishes his material to convey. Along with
praise, gnomic reflections play an important role within the
epinician song, pointing out the relevance of the particular event

[6] Cf. Silk, op.cit. for a discussion of the devices Pindar employs to join together
literal and figurative levels of speech.

[7] The presence of concrete detail is emphasised by H. Lloyd-Jones, 'Modern
interpretation of Pindar, the *2nd Pythian* and *7th Nemean Odes*', *JHS* 93 (1973),
pp.109-37.

to all men and satisfying the didactic role that poetry also fills.
Gnomic material exists within the discrete metaphoric
expression, where such symbols as the Pillars of Heracles serve as
reminders of the limits all mortals must observe so as not to
provoke the anger of the gods (N. 3.21). The brevity of human
happiness appears in the shape of the tree at P. 8.92-4, where
delight grows only to fall to the ground, shaken by an *apotropôi
gnômai*, a remorseless decree. The moral reflections Pindar
includes form part of the wider themes and theses that lie
directly beneath the surface of the odes, both in the particular
metaphor and the larger process of symbolisation that the poet
contrives. The metaphoric expression provides a model of how
the poem leads us towards its conceptual levels, and reveals the
particular thoughts and notions of the individual poet. Thematic
material becomes apparent when we seek to replace the
metaphor with a paraphrase. Literal meaning and 'virtual'
language cannot be recreated by an exact translation of the
words alone since metaphor and symbolic representation
transform the material, creating a novel composite for which no
literal term exists. The first meaning of the metaphor relates to a
known field of reference, the second to one for which there is no
direct characterisation. The impossibility of achieving a direct
match between the explicans and the explicandum, whether in
the individual metaphor or the overall presentation of the
subject, forces the audience not merely to elucidate but to
interpret.[8] The first act, which seeks to determine the contextual
meaning of a group of words given both their standard sense and
the range of connotation they possess, is insufficient and
interpretation alone can discover the relations between the words
and themes or theses. It examines the individual expression at
the level of the sentence, the stanza or the poem as a whole in
attempting to establish its place within the system of meaning
the poet constructs. Thus metaphor and symbolism provide a
means of entry into the dense conceptual material the Pindaric
ode contains. Each of Pindar's metaphors is a synthesis, evoking
the missing and the present parts of its range of meaning, resting
on the suspended as well as the displayed reference. The poem
does not directly state its theme, but permits the audience access

---

[8] Beardsley, op.cit., p.401f. for differences between elucidation and
interpretation.

to its meaning through the construction of layer upon layer of associated sense.

Themes and content both relate directly to the structure of the ode, in part determined by the demands of the genre, in part by the poet's own individual choice. The poem proceeds through a variety of devices in order to include all necessary elements, and to preserve the laudandus always near the centre of its course. Pindar uses structures which are sometimes conventional, sometimes of the poet's own invention. The odes progress through priamels and foils, climaxes and diminuendos in order to focus the full light of praise on the victor.[9] These conventional frames rest on relations of polarity and analogy, setting the subject in line with other characters and events in patterns of likeness and unlike. The use of these methods implicitly reinforces the praise; victory, Pindar's devices would suggest, is so magnificent a thing that it defies direct account and can only be approached by oblique means. Superlatives drawn from other realms describe the multifaceted nature of its excellence, demonstrating how it may sustain comparison with the ideal any other area promotes.[10] Metaphor also contributes to the structure of the ode independent of the particular convention in which it is placed. It fills a double function, reinforcing coherence between the individual portions of the poem in creating echoes of sound and sense, and building bridges between one unit and the next. A single metaphoric motif may dominate an entire ode; *P*. 2 is remarkable for the quantity of beast imagery it contains, while symbols of light and water recur throughout *N*. 7. Sometimes the provenance of a metaphor may be apparent, demonstrating how Pindar keeps his immediate subject present throughout the wider themes he treats. Wrestling imagery enters no fewer than six of the twelve stanzas of *N*. 4, as suits a song composed to celebrate a victory in the ring. Structure and thematic material coincide as the development of a particular motif parallels the ode's course from start to finish. *P*. 3 opens with a mention of Asclepius as craftsman, practitioner

---

[9] Terms devised by Bundy, op.cit. and, in part, developed from W. Schadewaldt, *Der Aufbau des pindarischen Epinikion* (Halle, 1928).

[10] B. Snell discusses the comparison as a descriptive device which enables men to give full expression to value and merit. *Die Entdeckung des Geistes*, 4th ed. (Göttingen, 1975), ch.11.

of the healing art (6). The image evolves into a vehicle for the contrast between skills which grant a temporary release from pain, and those whose powers of healing and preservation are eternal. Metaphors and symbols which appear at the very beginning of a poem can await resolution until the end, contributing to the ring structure an ode may follow. Metaphors of excellence appear in the opening lines of *O*. 1 (1-7), and return again in the final epode of the song (113-14). Metaphor also suggests movement from one theme or kind of material to another. In the absence of any obvious bridge between two portions, Pindar uses the literal language of one unit as metaphor in another. The vocabulary of horsemanship appears in the first two stanzas of *O*. 3, although the second verse describes not victory in the horse race, but Pindar's fulfilment of his poetic task. The poet describes himself in terms of harness and yoke (4-7):

> Μοῖσα δ᾽ οὕτω ποι παρέ-
> στα μοι νεοσίγαλον εὑρόντι τ᾽ρόπον
> Δωρίῳ φωνὰν ἐναρμόξαι πεδίλῳ
> ἀγ᾽λαόκωμον· ἐπεὶ χαίταισι μὲν
> ζευχθέντες ἔπι στέφανοι
> πράσσοντί με τοῦτο θεόδ᾽ματον χρέος,

The Muse stood by me while I found a new-shining way to harness the splendid choral voice to the Dorian measure, when, wreaths fastened about my hair, this god-given duty urged me on.

Frequently the metaphoric expression itself describes the links between the portions as Pindar selects those images best able to match the changing subject matter of the poem at that point. The difficulty of the epinician art lies precisely in building smooth joints between the different units, fixing naming elements to praise, praise to gnome, gnome to myth. The points of passage make demands on the poet's skill, and Pindar introduces metaphors which refer to strength and sleight of hand and limb at just those moments when he must cross a divide.[11] The athlete struggling in the contest (*N*. 7.70-3), the helmsman

[11] F.J. Nisetich, *Pindar's Victory Odes* (Baltimore, 1980), p.26.

seeking to master his vessel (*P.* 10.51-2), point to the poet
striving to create a passage between the parts of his song.
Metaphors of motion likewise describe the transition from
portion to portion. Descriptions of figurative stops and starts, of
journey's beginning and journey's ending impose divisions on
subject and theme, as Pindar signals his intention to move on
with a metaphor of embarkation (e.g. *P.* 2.62).[12] Frequently the
language of travel and that of poetic narration coincide, and at
N. 4.69-72 the poet moves easily from the tale of far-flung
voyages to his own treatment of his subject matter:

> Γαδείρων τὸ πρὸς ζόφον οὐ περατόν· ἀπότ'ρεπε
> αὖτις Εὐρώπαν ποτὶ χέρσον ἔντεα ναός·
> ἄπορα γὰρ λόγον Αἰακοῦ
> παίδων τὸν ἄπαντά μοι διελθεῖν.

Into the dark mist of Gadeira one may not pass. Turn back
again the sails of the ship towards Europe, the dry land.
There are no means for me to go through the whole tale of
the children of Aeacus.

Apora picks up *peraton*, and *dielthein* returns to the idea of
passage which the first image evoked. The motion which the
metaphors describe reflects the actual rearrangements going on
at the level of material and themes as Pindar builds meaning
even into the frame which holds the ode together.

Pindaric metaphor thus addresses every facet of the poem, its
context, contents, themes and structure. It can be approached at
a number of levels, but always involves multiple relations with
the overall design of the ode. It may be viewed as a specific
device of praise, celebrating the fortunes of the poet's patron by
comparing his glory to excellence or lack of merit in other
spheres. It may be understood as a generalising, moralising
figure which extends the significance of the poet's words from the
particular man to the collective audience and makes the
individual experience relevant to all. The metaphor not only
serves as a vehicle for theses and themes, but allows Pindar to

---

[12] For a good account of travel metaphors as structuring devices see J. Péron,
Les Images maritimes de Pindare (Paris, 1974), particularly the opening and
concluding chapters.

pass from one source of praise to another, from one reflection to the next. While all metaphoric expressions share in certain common features, combining literal and figurative levels of meaning, interaction between the parts and a transformation of the original sense of tenor and vehicle, different groups of metaphor in Pindar highlight different facets of his art. The poet's imagery can be seen not only in terms of its contribution to the particular genre, but as the means through which he individualises his medium, and makes it the vessel for his original insights. The categories of metaphor that Pindar selects are key to the poet's understanding of his own art, and create the framework within which he chooses to set both laudator and laudandus.

3

Of Plants and Men

The purpose of encomiastic verse is to preserve human glory at
its height, and to arrest the process of decline, decay and
forgetfulness which characterises mortal lives. The ode must not
only outlast its maker and its subject, but continue to live and
grow within the minds of men. Pindar views the victory in its
most perishable aspects, as the briefest moment of rapid bloom
within a fleeting existence, and seeks to give it lasting form. The
symbols of natural vegetation, of the Muses and Graces, and of
craftsmanship all belong to a complex of imagery which
describes the transient victory in relation to the permanent song,
and establishes a mid-point between growth and decline which
will hold the moment of brilliance for all time.

The image of plant life serves as a good introduction to
Pindar's use of metaphor, taking in the many roles that
figurative language plays within the verse. Like so many
Pindaric metaphors, it emerges naturally from the context of the
Games, suggested by the crown of leaves which the triumphant
athlete wore. In promoting encomium, metaphors of vegetation
provide terms of comparison and contrast to the victor's
achievement, acting now as a mirror to, now as a foil for, his
fortunes. They are a vehicle for moralising as well as praise; the
regeneration of leaf and blossom each spring encourages the
subject and the audience of the song to look for fresh glory, while
the inevitable decay all plant life undergoes warns the individual
against placing too much confidence in present good. Such
gnomic reflections universalise the impact of the victor's
experience and the poet's word, and point to the thematic
material the symbol also carries. The plant metaphor is an
important one in addressing the poet-victor relationship,
describing the interaction of the laudandus and his song, and the
particular effect of one upon the other. The task of the poet is to

participate in his subject's experience, and Pindar and his verse appear within the same complex of vegetational imagery as the patron and his achievements. However, the very coincidence of the imagery is used to draw a critical distinction between the plant-like aspects of human life and those of song; while one is transient, the other endures, and the blossom of poetry is one that, uniquely, does not fade or fall. Pindar creates, through the fusion of the realms of vegetation and of song, a particular flower which exists in the poetic realm alone, combining permanence and change, nature and the poet's art.

In *Iliad* 6.146f., Homer compares the life and death of mortal men with the natural process of growth and wilting of leaves on a tree: 'The generations of men are like those of leaves. Some leaves the wind sheds upon the earth, while others the flourishing forest puts forth while the season of spring is at hand.' The analogy between plant and human life is a traditional one, and continues through lyric poetry where Semonides echoes the Homeric simile (29.2), and Mimnermus builds about the same theme (2.1f.).[1] The natural sequence of growth, blossom and decay provides the poet with a ready image for the passage from life to death which all men experience, and, through traditional language and imagery, Pindar establishes a close match between the progress which plants and mortal men describe. The thematic material which the analogy is made to bear belongs both to the concerns of the epinician genre, and to the idividual poet alone. Pindar follows the birth, growth and development of his human subjects through the vocabulary the plant world suggests; the language of young life establishes an early identification between men and vegetation, and Greek terms for the infant or child belong equally to plant and human contexts; Pindar describes his athletes and heroes with such common terms as *thalos*, young branch and *ernos*, shoot (e.g. *O.* 2.45; *O.* 6.68; *N.* 6.37; *I.* 3/4.63), and calls Iamos the *theophrôn kouros*, godly-minded youth or twig as he emerges, shoot-like, from the dark coppice where his mother gives birth (*O.* 6.40-1). Cities and islands likewise grow in the language plant life provides. *O.* 7 traces the progress of Rhodes from the depths of the sea where it lies seed-like and dormant, and witnesses its

---

[1] On the question of Semonides' use of the Homeric conceit see H. Lloyd-Jones, *Females of the Species* (London, 1975), Appendix I.

growth beneath the fostering rays of the sun (61f.). The city's original population springs from the union between the earth and the fertilising rays of the sun, an image for the process of generation in plants (70f.).[2]

The advent of spring within the lives of plants and cities follows on their initial growth, as Pindar continues to draw parallels between the different realms. He uses the terminology of plant life to describe the young boy's passage into youth. While the plant puts out leaves in the springtime, Pelops grows a beard (*O*. 1.67-8) and Iamos acquires the fruit of gold-crowned Hebe (*O*. 6.57-8). The identification between youth, blossom, fruit and flower is so frequent in lyric poetry that the term *hêbês anthos*, flower of youth, becomes virtually a poetic cliché, signalling in one the bursting forth that young vegetation and young life display in their respective springtimes.[3] Leaves, fruits and blossoms in Pindar are all symbols for virtue and triumph in the Games and in other spheres as the poet projects the achievement he celebrates onto the broadest backdrop that nature can provide. At their moment of victory in battle or athletics, men burst into bloom (*N*. 4.88; *N*.9.39) or cull the fruits of their merit and worth (*O*. 1.13). Young girls at their height of loveliness appear in the form of flowers, and Pindar describes men's desire to pluck them at this point (*P*. 9.109-11). The city likewise enjoys rejuvenation in the springtime in the shape of the actual return of vegetation and through the flowers that play an important role in the spring festivals which celebrate renewed fertility and those gods held responsible for new growth. Spring promotes the appearance of the leaves from which the citizens may weave wreaths for honouring the gods in celebrations which give thanks both for the temporary fertility and the enduring blossoms which the immortals bestow upon men (Fr. 52a.5-10).

The symbol of the flower of youth carries with it a poignant note, evoking the transient character of any beauty or brilliance at its peak. Pindar portrays success as a fleeting thing, no more lasting than the youthful prowess and loveliness of the boy who

---

[2] The vegetational metaphor is seen as a key to the unity of *O*. 7 by D.C. Young, 'Three odes of Pindar: a literary study of *Pythian 11*, *Pythian 3*, and *Olympian 7*', *Mnemosyne* Suppl.9 (1968), pp.69-105.

[3] Silk op.cit., p.100.

has won the greatest prize. Pindaric heroes are fully aware of the need to act before the passage of their youth, and Pelias draws the contrast between his own old age, and Jason, in his youthful prime:

> ἤδη με γηραιὸν μέρος ἁλικίας
> ἀμφιπολεῖ· σὸν δ᾽ ἄνθος ἥβας ἄρτι κυ-
> μαίνει·

(P. 4.157-8)

Already that portion of life, old age, attends on me. But in you the flower of youth is now swelling.

The transitory character of victory in the Games is part of the broader nature of impermanence which stamps all human happiness and good fortune. The very essence of beauty and youth lies with its perishability, and its rapid passage may be compared to the swift growth and decay of leaves upon the tree (Mimnermus 2.1). The flower is the central symbol in Pindar and Sappho's representation of young men and women who possess the beauty, freshness, delicacy and perishability which combine to create 'youth', that brief moment when loveliness shines out with its full radiance.[4] Like the flower, fruit or leaf, human delight and prowess, focused within the springtime youth, is the thing of an instant, vulnerable to the slightest change in time or conditions:

> ἐν δ᾽ ὀλίγῳ βροτῶν
> τὸ τερπνὸν αὔξεται· οὕτω δὲ καὶ πίτνει χαμαί,
> ἀποτ'ρόπῳ γνώμᾳ σεσεισμένον.

(P. 8.92-4)

In a short moment men's delight grows strong. In a short moment too it falls to the ground, shaken by an implacable intention.

Pindar deliberately evokes images of passing brilliance in order to establish the contrast between them and his symbols of

---

[4] For further discussion of Sappho's use of the flower as symbol of youth see T. McEvilley, 'Sapphic imagery and Fragment 96', *Hermes* 101 (1973), pp.257-78.

decay and devastation. Whether the natural process of decline sets in, or whether some more violent check intrudes, metaphors describing the destruction of fruits and flowers permit Pindar to construct the necessary foil to triumph in every sphere. Perhaps the most familiar conceit of all, building on the earlier conjunction, is that of the flower of youth cut down in its prime. Pindar portrays youth's perishable blossom when he speaks of Diodotus who lost his life on the field of battle, *euanthe' apepneusas halikian*, having breathed out his flowering youth (*I.* 7.34). A fragment similarly describes the death of young men *thallontes hêbai*, in their bloom of youth (Fr. 171). The poet uses the same elements which cast down crops and fruits to represent the devastation of human fortunes, projecting the vocabulary of the natural elements into men's lives where reversals take the active shape of rain, clouds and stormy skies. Fair weather promotes the lives of plants, men and cities, while foul threatens them, and the metaphor of clouds and storms appears frequently in a figurative capacity in the odes. The traditional symbol of the storm of war deprives a household of its offspring at *I.* 3/4.35, and the city needs two anchors to resist the threatening weather (*O.* 6.100-1). Even when men escape the hostile forces Nature directs against them, they undergo eventual decline. The same conditions make for the decay of men and plants as they mark a parallel course; while the tree sheds its leaves and the flower droops, the old man becomes bent and bald.[5] The darkness and the dryness that men must face as they come close to death are the negation of the light and moisture which foster natural growth.

Against his gloomy backdrop of rapid blossom, and the quick onset of decline which overcomes the fruit and flower of happiness, Pindar sets a possible alternative. Plant life does not merely trace a linear course from birth to blossom, but is part of a larger cycle which involves death and regeneration, periods of fertility and times of fallow. The metaphor of plant life enables the poet to establish a variation to the theme of passage from life to death, and one which will directly involve the role of the epinician song and the circumstances of its composition. By comparing plant to mortal progress, Pindar paints fortunes that may come and go, and suggests that decline is a necessary

---

[5] Aeschylus, *Agamemnon*, 79f.

prelude to future flowering. To his athlete or patron he holds out
the hope of a renewal of fortune, and of the future victory which
he may yet achieve. The cycle of the seasons, and the circling
course of the years serve as a metaphor for the regeneration of
glory:

> τεκμαίρει {δὲ} καί νυν Ἀλκιμίδας τὸ συγγενὲς ἰδεῖν
> ἄγχι καρποφόροις ἀρούραισιν, αἵτ᾽ ἀμειβόμεναι
> τόκα μὲν ὧν βίον ἀνδράσιν ἐπ-
> ηετανὸν ἐκ πεδίων ἔδοσαν,
> τόκα δ᾽ αὖτ᾽ ἀναπαυσάμεναι σθένος ἔμαρψαν

(*N.* 6.8-11)

And now Alcimidas too attests that the power of kinship is
like the fruit-bearing fields which, in turn, at one time give
yearly sustenance to men from the earth, at another rest,
gathering strength.

Youth, within this scheme, need not be lost forever, but, like the
springtime, will inevitably return through the passage of the
seasons. While Hora herself is the goddess of the prime of youth,
the springtime blossom in a mortal life, the collective Horae
preside over the cycle of time and the seasonal round. They are
the deities who, at *O.* 4.1-3, perform a circling dance. The
festivities which they likewise possess a recurrent
nature, returning each year in due season. The cyclical motion of
the individual year belongs within the broader pattern of the
circular motion time describes, where the passage of the ages is
seen not as a linear but a ring composition. At *N.* 11.37f., Pindar
evokes the notion of years that return in his metaphor of the fruit
trees which yield their crop not annually, but every other year,
an image for the varying fortunes a family experiences:

> ἀρχαῖαι δ᾽ ἀρεταί
> ἀμφέροντ᾽ ἀλλασσόμεναι γενεαῖς ἀνδρῶν σθένος·
> ἐν σχερῷ δ᾽ οὔτ᾽ ὧν μέλαιναι καρπὸν ἔδωκαν ἄρουραι,
> δένδρεά τ᾽ οὐκ ἐθέλει πάσαις ἐτέων περόδοις
> ἄνθος εὐῶδες φέρειν πλούτῳ ἴσον

Ancient excellences bring forth men's strength, alternating in generations. The dark fields do not yield fruit continuously, nor are the trees willing in the cycle of years to bring out fragrant flowers equal in wealth, but in alternation.

The chance of renewed growth also lies within the character of the plant itself. The leaf, branch or flower is no isolated object, but part of a larger organism which will endure. Some parts of the plant and tree resist destruction and the natural process of decay; the root proves more durable than the growth above ground, and anchors the tree firmly to the place where first it grew.[6] Roots, like the other attributes of Pindaric vegetation, also belong to humankind, and remain while the branches, shoots and leaves may be cut off. The plant becomes a vital symbol within the Pindaric theme of the continuing life of the family, and the heritage which is so critical a part of the makeup of the individual man. Growing from the ancestral stock, the new sprig chances to inherit some of the qualities which distinguished his divine, mythical and historical ancestors, those individuals who form a central part of the victor's lasting fame, and deserve mention and celebration in the ode. The excellence that the present-day laudandus displays is, in part, the result of his glorious descent, and the merit a family enjoys reaches from its roots to its subsequent flowering in the Games. Pindar establishes continuity between the original growth and present bloom in his descriptions of his victor, sprung from the ancestral root (*O.* 2.46), and elsewhere speaks of the glory which deeds of prowess bring to the family stock (*I.* 8.56). Roots also belong to the city in which the victor dwells, and the symbol enables Pindar to explore the notion of the bonds that exist between a man and the land which forms an integral part of his nature. Cities originally grow from roots (*P.* 4.14-16). These lie buried within the soil which fosters the seed of the unborn athlete and houses the heroes of the past and the eponymous city Nymph. The city root also symbolises the hope of stability and regeneration, and its continuing life resembles that of a tree. The

[6] The importance of roots in Greek tradition may be derived from very early notions of the world as a tree, anchored to the ground by its roots. For further discussion of the 'world tree' see M. West, *Early Greek Philosophy and the Orient* (Oxford, 1971), p.55f. and U. Holmberg, *Der Baum des Lebens* (Helsinki, 1922).

victor, in gaining his triumph, reveals the original sources of life which normally lie hidden beneath the ground, and his own flowering promotes the fertility of his land.[7] The city enjoys rejuvenation through the garlands which its citizens bring back from their triumphs in the Games, and their victories generate *thalia* in the city, a term which describes both communal rejoicing and natural fertility (*O.* 7.93-4).[8]

In his metaphors which set together the lives of plants and men, Pindar draws in characteristic fashion on likeness and difference, establishing parallels and antitheses which prepare the way for the role of song. The poet, although he offers hope for renewed growth in men's fortunes, simultaneously exposes the brevity of mortal life. Human time is not the cyclical one which the gods and Nature observe, but linear in character, describing a path from life to death beneath the dictates of the Moirae. The Fates lead men on towards the moment of their death, back towards the soil where they began, and Pindar's references to the goddesses serve as a reminder of man's inevitable mortality.[9] The use of the nature metaphor creates a telling contrast between plant and human existence, even in the middle of the parallels which Pindar draws. Each man, according to his formulation, has only one lifetime and one brief spring in which to earn his *kleos*, that fame which alone enables the individual to escape the mortal time scale, and join a more enduring one.

It is in the matter of a man's *kleos* that the poet's art comes into play. His task as the composer of epinician songs is to transform the brief bloom of human success into durable stuff, and to ensure that the laudandus' fame will be recalled. Pindar prepares the way for this description of poetic power in metaphors which make vegetation of the song. The act of composition involves growth, bloom and fruitfulness as Pindar creates *phull' aoidan*, leaves of song, (*I.* 3/4.45) and a *thalos aoidan*, sprig of song (Fr. 70a.14). He uses the context of the Games to justify the metaphor of plant life, likening the ode to

---

[7] For an explanation of the literal quality of these so-called metaphors see D.S. Carne-Ross, 'Root, tree, flower: a Pindaric path of thought', printed as an appendix to 'Weaving with points of gold: Pindar's *Sixth Olympian*', *Arion*, n.s. 3/1 (1976), pp. 42-4..

[8] The interchangeability of *thalia* and *thallia* is pointed out by Young, op.cit., pp.96-7.

[9] W. Mullen, *Choreia: Pindar and Dance* (Princeton, 1982), p.218.

the crown of leaves which the triumphant victor receives, the only apparent recompense for his pains. The athlete after claiming his prize would proceed beneath a shower of flowers and of leaves, the *phyllobolia* or pelting with leaves which Pindar's own songs imitate (*P.* 8.57).[10] The metaphor of the wreath of song is a powerful one in describing the conjunction of natural life and the permanence which poetry promotes. It brings together the garland, symbol of transience, and speech, which, by virtue of the truth and powers of disclosure it contains, bears its fruits unceasingly over time. The act of crowning with song spans the realms of the living and the dead; it may describe the garlanding of the present-day athlete which is announced to the dead (*O.* 14.20-4) or refer to the poet and chorus who crown themselves as they relate the athlete's spring that follows on the dead man's wintery storm (*I.* 7.27f.). The ode, through naming the athlete's historical and mythical ancestors, recreates their moment of triumph and blossom when they too received the flowers of victory in the Games or in battle. In juxtaposing evocations of the dead with the image of the crown of leaves, the ode points to its own ability permanently to re-enact the actual ceremony of crowning that the living victor passes through. The song, in addition to prevailing over the passage of time, withstands the challenge of the forces which threaten man-as-plant, fostering the bloom and fruitfulness of the laudandus. The virtue or success which the individual achieves appears as the plant which the song of praise nourishes, dispensing the essential life and water which create the conditions for its growth. At *N.* 8.40f., Pindar portrays the close relationship between the two:

ἀἰσσει δ' ἀρετά, χλωραῖς ἐέρσαις
  ὡς ὅτε δένδρεον ⟨– –⟩,
⟨ἐν⟩ σοφοῖς ἀνδρῶν ἀερθεῖσ' ἐν δικαίοις τε πι'ρὸς ὑγρόν
αἰθέρα.

Excellence grows upwards, like a tree in the fresh dews, raised up towards the moist air among men who are wise and just.

---

[10] On the practice of *phyllobolia* see E. Borthwick, 'Zoologica Pindarica', *CQ* n.s. 26 (1976), p.198f. and Pfeiffer ad Callimachus 260.13 in R. Pfeiffer, *Callimachus* (Oxford, 1949), p.247.

Although the blossom of song originally depends on the victor's deed, it will then promote its further growth within this and subsequent generations. The bloom of poetry is a lasting one, capable of renewed flowering. At the close of *O.* 6, Pindar asks the god Poseidon that he may give 'growth to the lovely flowers of song', songs of the future which the poet will compose in response to new victories (104-5). The individual poem is also a cyclical thing, and Pindar terms his Paeans *horiai* (Fr. 128c.2), indicating the seasonal character of works which are performed at recurrent festivals and regular Games. The ode does not end with the death of the man whom it praises, but its own blossom preserves him in the memory of those who hear the song.

Pindar's combination of the very different categories of natural vegetation and of poetry transforms the character of both. The plant life which the songs emulate passes beyond the natural context, and the sequence of growth and decay that crops and flowers on earth must follow. They become a part of the vegetation which belongs to divine and idyllic spheres, taking their unique character from their place of origin, and from the divinities who oversee their growth. The flowers which Pindar bestows are the gift of the Graces (*O.* 2.50-1), and the Seasons themselves bring the poet to the site where he will make his wreaths of verse (*O.* 4.1-3). Pindar's songs do not grow in the ordinary gardens and fields of men, but in the meadows of the Muses where the poet goes in search of inspiration and true material. He portrays himself in these haunts as the gardener and ploughman of an eternally fertile soil, tending and plucking his songs of praise (*O.* 9.26; *P.* 6.1-2). These gardens belong to the alternative vegetation which flourishes in the lands of gods and favoured men who have achieved a state of quasi-immortality. In these settings, the land of the Golden Age, Elysium, and the Islands of the Blessed, the lives of plants and men do coincide since the vegetation is not wholly natural nor men quite mortal. Pindar expresses his notion of the lasting renown which a man may achieve in terms of the undying vegetation of his song, creating a Hesiodic Golden Age of permanence which represents an escape from the cycle of both earth-bound plant and human life.

In these idealised lands, the natural processes of growth and decay do not operate, but the plants are forever in bloom and the

season eternal springtime.[11] The same remarkable trees and
flowers are to be found in the Islands of the Blessed (*O*. 1.71-2)
and in the *Threnos* where Pindar speaks of the:

φοινικορόδοις ⟨δ'⟩ ἐνὶ λειμώνεσσι προάστιον αὐτῶν
καὶ λιβάνων σκιαρᾶν ⟨   ⟩
καὶ χρυσοκάρποισιν βέβριθε ⟨δενδρέοις⟩

(Fr. 129.3-5)

meadows of scarlet roses in the city outskirts, shaded by
frankincense, and weighed down with golden fruits.

Gold figures prominently in both accounts, symbolising fixity in
a metal which does not fade or decay. It represents the artificial
continuum of song in contrast with the natural cycle of life and
death which the growth and fall of leaves from a tree convey. The
Muses wear wreaths of gold about their heads (*P*. 3.89), and
the semi-divine Hyperboreans dance and revel with golden
bay-leaves in their hair (*P*. 10.40).[12] The song does not merely
suspend the vegetal cycle, but arrests and represents it at its
height of bloom. The *kleos* that it sings is truly *aphthiton*, an
epithet which negates decay and may describe the permanent
and sacred order of the Olympians with whom the individual is
incorporated after death through the medium of epic or the
epinician.[13]

Pindar's use of the metaphor of plant life to describe his song
provides a perspective not merely on the epinician ode, but on
the wider poetic process, and the role of the symbol within it.
The conjunction of poetry and flower runs throughout
discussions of the poetic imagination, and the transformations
which it effects on the linguistic medium. For Coleridge, plant
and flower life are a means of representing the metaphoric
exchange through which the life of the individual and that of the
surrounding world grow together, the process which Pindar as

[11] The link between perpetual vegetation and undying existence is explored by
G. Nagy in *The Best of the Achaeans* (Baltimore, 1979).
[12] On the symbolism of the golden wreath in Pindar see J. Duchemin, 'Essai sur
le symbolisme Pindarique: or, lumière et couleurs', *REG* 65 (1952), p.56.
[13] G. Nagy, op.cit., ch.10 and idem, *Comparative Studies in Greek and Indic
Meter* (Cambridge, Mass., 1974).

poet and celebrant of a particular man's triumph describes. The growth of plants serves as a symbol for metaphoric transfer and exchange, and the window they provide upon a higher truth; as the plant reaches towards the light and into the earth, and draws its growth from both, it 'upholds the ceaseless plastic motion of the parts in the profoundest rest of the whole; it becomes the visible *organismus* of the whole silent or elementary life of nature and therefore, in incorporating the one extreme becomes the symbol of the other'.[14] While describing the interaction between the parts of the metaphor, its fusion of the particular with the general, the symbol of the plant or flower also describes the natural life and motion of poetic speech. Song, when seen as a part of vegetational growth, belongs to nature, and to *phusis*, that process of generation which permits creativity in both art and life. Pindar's verse is a thing of both *phusis* and *poiêsis* as the poet presides over the song's blossoming and growth by its own impetus.[15] Metaphor promotes the act, quickening the latent motion of the word or object. Heidegger, like Coleridge, evokes the symbol of the flower and blossom as a metaphor for metaphor, focusing both on the unity of being it represents, and on the actual process of creation it involves. Thus the flowers of our words – *Worte wie Blumen* – utter existence in breaking forth, emerging into their proper being.[16] In permanently re-enacting this moment of blossom, the word stands as a lasting testimonial to the athlete's flower, and establishes fixity within the very act of motion.

---

[14] Quoted in Richards, op.cit., p.111.

[15] Aristotle defines the term *phusis* as '1. The genesis of growing things, 2. that immanent part of a growing thing, from which its growth first proceeds, 3. the source from which the primary movement in each natural object is present in it by virtue of its own essence ...' He continues: 'From what has been said, then, it is plain that nature in the primary and strict sense is the essence of things which have in themselves, as such, a source of movement.' (*Metaphysics* D4. 1014b16-1015a15).

[16] M. Heidegger, *On the Way to Language* (trans. Peter D. Hertz, New York, 1971), pp.99-100.

4

Truth and Beauty

Pindar's metaphors of vegetational growth naturally involve those deities most intimately concerned with the lives of plants and flowers. While continuing the theme of the transient loveliness of blossom and fruitfulness, Pindar introduces an element of the divine to his floral symbols, an element which further guarantees the permanence of the bloom of song. Fittingly, the immortals who oversee natural fertility also have a vital role to play within the poet's own task, and preside over creativity both in nature and in art. Poetry is no isolated undertaking, but an act which requires external aid for both its composition and performance. The poet traditionally invokes Apollo, supreme lord of poetry, and more particularly the Muses who serve as the source of his poetic identity and of his inspiration. The Muses take their place in Pindar alongside the other groups of female deities, the Graces and the Seasons, who play a distinctive role in the creation of song and its delivery to the victorious athlete. The powers and attributes of these divine creatures become those of the poet in the practice of his craft, and he enjoys access to the world of natural luxuriance and fertility in which they dwell. The same deities leave their regular environment to accompany the song to the place of performance. The Muses and Graces assume the role of *kômos*, lending an enduring character to a momentary event as they merge their identity with the band of revellers who welcome the athlete to his native city and perform the epinician song. They bring their characteristic pastimes of music, celebration and dance into the city sphere where they continue to fulfil their life-promoting role. Their powers in the realm of nature find expression in the part the song can play in the growth of the community, while their own divine character ensures that the glory that the poet sings will be a lasting one.

The relationship between the poet and his Muses changes in

the course of Greek poetry, and their role in Pindar is a combination of tradition and innovation characteristic of the poet's metaphors.[1] In Homer, the Muses act as the indispensable source of material, the daughters of Mnemosyne who give the poet access to accurate information concerning the past, present and future events which he sings. In the prologue of the *Theogony*, the Muses' role is more an inspirational than a purely didactic one. Changed by their intervention which appears as an epiphany and initiation, the poet himself gains in stature, a character at once more sacred and individualised than in the Homeric poems. In Pindar, although many of the poems begin by acknowledging the inspiration that the singer owes to his Muses, the poet's own talent receives increased emphasis. He portrays the equality of participation in metaphors which claim a parity in roles and possessions; the poet who celebrates the *kleos* of mortal men imitates the activity of the Muses who sing the *genos*, the race and geneology, of the gods on Mount Olympus. In composing his verse, Pindar mounts the chariot of the divine patronesses, and uses the bow which delivers their arrows of song (*O. 9.5*). The poet is even of a stature to give the Muses instructions, requesting that they direct a breeze of song towards a particular victor (*N. 6.28*). The Muses no longer furnish the actual material of the verse, but rather the element of talent or skill necessary for its composition, the *sophia* which in Pindar may denote creative ability, technical skill and inventiveness.[2] The poem remains the joint creation of this gift and the poet's nature. Pindar often portrays song as the product of his own spirit, and mingles the divine with the human contribution when he refers to the ode as the 'Muses' gift, sweet fruit of my mind' (*O. 7-8*). No longer the principal force behind the composition, the Muses may function as pure metaphor, no more than a shorthand for the song. (*I. 6.2-3*; *P. 4.67*). The term *Mousa* permits Pindar to vary his means of expressing the theme of the athlete celebrated through the poet's verse. The Graces serve in a similar capacity to the Muses, at once actual deities who possess

---

[1] On the changing relationship between Muses and poets see J. de Romilly, 'Gorgias et le pouvoir de la poésie', *JHS* 93 (1973), p.157f., and the relevant entries in R.G.M. Nisbet and M. Hubbard, *A Commentary on Horace: Odes Book I* (Oxford, 1970).

[2] Cf. D. Gerber, *Pindar's Olympian I: A Commentary* (Toronto, 1982) at line 9, p.28.

distinctive roles in the making of song, and an additional term for portraying the song and its effect upon the man it celebrates. The Graces' contribution to the finished product complements that of the kindred Muses; while the latter are associated with Memory (*N.* 7.12-16) and with Truth (*O.* 10.3-4), acting as guarantors of the accuracy of Pindar's account, the former appear in the company of Aphrodite, of the Loves (Fr. 128) and Persuasion (Fr. 123.14). The company they keep indicates their ability to promote the beauty and persuasiveness of the ode, and they represent the loveliness with which Pindar hopes to invest his song. They carry with them the notion of brilliance and beauty which the floral metaphors described, but their radiance is of divine provenance, making of poetry a force which may dazzle and enchant. The Graces, like the Muses, also function as symbols for song or for the glory which surrounds the victor at his moment of triumph or of celebration (*O.* 7.11-12). Beyond the world of the individual poet, Muses and Graces involve themselves in all acts of artistic creation, and are sources of the *sophismata* without which no artist, sculptor, poet or philosopher can accomplish his task.[3]

Traditionally the Muses and the Graces are concerned less with the artistic sphere than with the world of nature where they promote fertility and fecundity in all living things. Pindar's choice of the term *zôthalmios*, giving the bloom of life, to describe Grace at *O.* 7.11 is no mere poetic conceit, but an attribute taken from the role of the immortals as personifications of life and growth within the natural environment. The worship of the goddesses in cult was designed to promote natural fertility, and mortals celebrated them in the hope that they would stimulate fruitfulness.[4] The Graces of Orchomenos, whom the poet makes the dominant motif of *Olympian* 14, were originally vegetational deities, while the flower-bearing Seasons whom he evokes at *O.* 13.17 often served as representatives of natural

---

[3] The cult of the Muses became a dominant theme among the philosophers of the fourth and fifth century. For further discussion see P. Boyancé, *Le Culte des Muses chez les philosophes grecs* (Paris, 1937).

[4] L. Farnell, *The Cults of the Greek States* vol.5 (Oxford, 1909), pp.434-7. Additional information may be found in W.F. Otto, *Die Musen und der göttliche Ursprung des Singens und Sagens* (Darmstadt, 1956) and relevant articles in W.H. Roscher, *Ausführliches Lexikon der griechischen und römischen Mythologie* (Leipzig 1884-1937).

abundance. The goddesses are portrayed holding fruits and flowers in literary and artistic accounts, visualisations of the annual rhythm of blossom and fruitfulness. These female groupings are responsible for human as well as plant life, and stimulate fertility in women, both mortal and divine; the Nymphs, close kin to the Muses, Graces and Seasons, have the sacred character of the *kourotrophoi*, child-rearers, and preside over the early infancy of Dionysus, Aristaeus and Zeus.[5] The places they frequent, the mountains, rivers, springs, trees and meadows of the Greek landscape, are frequently the birth places of the gods, of Artemis and Apollo among others, as though the natural fertility of the environment promoted the fertility of those who passed through it.[6] Their character as nature dwellers is an essential part of the identity of the goddesses who assume various shapes and forms according to their environment. Erato appears as both Muse and Nereid or water spirit, and, in Boeotia, Nymphs and Muses both shared the cult title *Libethriae*.[7] The Muses inhabit mountain tops and dance about springs. The opening lines of the *Theogony* provide evidence of their natural habit when Hesiod invokes the creatures who 'inhabit the great and sacred mountain of Helicon and dance on tender feet about the dark spring' (2-4).

Poets, in attributing their creative powers to these nature goddesses, participate in the natural forces they represent. The intellectual gifts which enter into the composition of songs are not divorced from the context of nature, but display similar powers of life, motion and fertility. The symbol of the Muses and Graces holds in one the twin forces which the song as flower describes, the *phusis* which indicates growth and movement, the *poiêsis*, which represents the poet's influence on the material. The metaphor of the goddesses complements that of the blossom of Pindar's song; it is in the garden of the Muses that the poet finds his flowers, the same place that would serve for the meditations of the philosopher and which combines the life of

---

[5] *Homeric Hymn* 26.3f.; Callimachus, *Hymn to Zeus*, 40f.

[6] On the meadow as a place of birth and generation see A. Motte, *Prairies et jardins dans la Grèce antique* (Brussels, 1971), pp.161-97. For rivers as *kourotrophoi* see R.B. Onians, *The Origins of European Thought* (Cambridge, 1951), p.229.

[7] Otto, op.cit., p.20.

nature and of the intellect.[8] The poet is a gardener, who tends the *exaireton Charitôn kapon*, choice garden of the Graces (*O.* 9.26). At *P.* 6.2, Pindar joins the other poets in ploughing the Muses' field which yields melodious crops. *Sophia* is also to be found within these haunts (*P.* 6.49). Poetry had long possessed an association with nature and its places of abundant fertility. In myth, Pan and Orpheus are both nature dwellers and the *zatheos leimôn*, sacred meadow, provides a backdrop to the competition between the two rival musicians, Hermes and Apollo.[9] Nature furnishes the poet with the tools of his craft, both actual and figurative symbols for poetic initiation. The singer accompanies himself on the reed pipe or the tortoise-shell lyre,[10] and within a natural setting the Muses meet the poet and present him with the laurel branch which marks his entry into the fraternity of bards.[11]

Initiation also signals inspiration, the transmission of creative forces from the Muses to their creature poets. Inspiration, as the term suggests, demands that the poet take in some power from without, and that he carry within him the force of the divine which makes him truly *entheos*, god-possessed.[12] The media which the Muses, Nymphs and Graces cohabit furnish natural symbols for the forces which the poet must accommodate; their presence is implied within water, the liquid substance which the singer often swallows.[13] The goddesses' epithet *Libethriae* evokes the watery element in which they sometimes dwell, and springs and fountains feed the plant life of their haunts, the meadows, gardens and Mount Helicon which Pausanias celebrates as the

---

[8] Motte, op.cit., pp.280-319.

[9] *Homeric Hymn*, 4.503.

[10] Ibid. 25, 47.

[11] The laurel branch as a symbol of poetic initiation receives detailed treatment in A. Kambylis, *Die Dichterweihe und ihre Symbolik* (Heidelberg, 1965).

[12] On inspiration see the discussion of Plato's third type of 'divine' madness, or 'possession by the Muses' in E.R. Dodds, *The Greeks and the Irrational* (Berkeley and Los Angeles, 1951), p.80f.

[13] The notion of inspiration which comes through some liquid medium, particularly sacred waters, is found in many cultures and traditions. For a general treatment see H.M. and N.K. Chadwick, *The Growth of Literature I* (Cambridge, 1932), p.648f. On its role in Greek concepts of inspiration, M. Ninck, *Die Bedeutung des Wassers im Kult und Leben der Alten* (repr. Darmstadt, 1960); H. Maehler, *Die Auffassung des Dichterberufs im frühen Griechentum bis zur Zeit Pindars* (Göttingen, 1963); and Kambylis, op.cit. Its particular uses in Pindar are listed in Péron, op.cit., p.234f.

most fertile place of all.[14] In Hesiod, the Muses dance about the waters of the fountain on Helicon and in Pindar they inhabit the Theban springs which act as the source of the poet's inspiration. These are the 'sacred waters of Dirce which the deep-girdled daughters of gold-robed Memory made to spring up beside the well-fortified gates of Cadmus' (*I*. 6.74-5). Nymphs also dwell in the waters of Thebes and Pindar addresses Metope:

> πλάξιππον ἁ Θήβαν ἔτι-
> κτεν, τᾶς ἐρατεινὸν ὕδωρ
> πίομαι

(*O*. 6.85-6)

whom horse-driving Thebes bore, from whose lovely water I drink.

In becoming the mouthpiece for a force beyond himself, the poet resembles the prophet who also looks to sacred waters for his inspiration.[15] Prophecy is the joint concern of Apollo and the Nymphs and Muses, and men possessed with prophetic fervour are termed *nympholêptoi*, caught by nymphs.[16] Holy fountains, according to Oenomaus, Lucian and their successors, inspired the Pythia who may have drunk from Castalia, the stream that descends the cleft at Delphi.[17] Another substance which the Muses share with the poet is honey; honey is the earthly counterpart to nectar, the Muses' gift (*O*. 7.7) and the food reserved for the immortal gods alone. The Muses and Nymphs receive honey offerings, *melikrata*, which testify to their chthonic character as well as to their role within the natural realm. A nymph, Melissa, was credited with first discovering the substance which later came to function as a symbol for the poet's initiation into his craft.[18] One late tradition relates how Pindar, as an infant, was anointed on the lips with honey, a presage of the sweetness that would come from his mouth.[19] Pindar

---

[14] Pausanias 9.28.1-4.
[15] H.W. Parke and D.E.W. Wormell, *The Delphic Oracle* (Oxford, 1956), p.27.
[16] L. Farnell, op.cit., p.425. According to Pausanias, Nymphs themselves possess powers of divination, and those who lived on Mount Cithaeron once gave out prophecies (9.3.9).
[17] Parke and Wormell, op.cit., p.27.
[18] Schol. ad *P*. 4.106.
[19] Pausanias 9.23.2.

imagines his song in the form of showers of honey as the poet delivers what he himself has taken in from his divine sources (*O.* 10.98). Honey too has a role in stimulating prophetic frenzy, and the Thriae, the bee maidens of the *Hymn to Hermes* who give out oracles, feed on the honeycomb.[20]

Through his metaphors of the poet's source of inspiration, and matching images for the song itself, Pindar attributes certain properties to his verse. Water shares in the qualities the Muses and Graces incarnate, freshness, brilliance and gentleness, also the cardinal features of song. Verse appeases the most turbulent of spirits in *P.* 1.10f., and soothes the athlete's tired limbs at *N.* 4.2-5. The importance of the element which Pindar celebrates as the best of substances lies with its vivifying and regenerative powers, and the liquid symbol brings to song the life-giving force of its divine inspirers. Moisture and the Muses promote natural vegetation, while Pindar sends down showers of praise on men and cities whose glory flourishes in response. In *O.* 10, a whole complex of imagery traces the relationship between poetry and fame, expressing the process through images which evoke water and the Muses. Fame, like a plant, grows beneath the soft shower which lyre and flute send down on it, and is tended by the Muses in their role as nurturers of all incipient life (93-6). The poet's honey-rain in the concluding stanza lends additional fertility to the city's soil, ensuring that the fame of Hagesidamus will find within it a constant source of nourishment, and that he will remain, in men's recall at least, 'fair to look at' in his youth (103-4). Water in the form of dew also acts as an agent of growth, and a metaphor for the poet's song at *P.* 5.99-100. The same image recurs at *N.* 8.40f. when Pindar describes the nurturing powers of praise through the metaphor of a tree's growth. The symbol of dew, like water and honey, is particularly apt: it evokes the sacred quality of a substance personified as Pandrosus, Nymph-like sister to Herse and Aglaurus and a cult figure worshipped in the Arrephoria where the three maidens' concern was with fertility.[21]

A further medium for the Muses and Graces is light,

---

[20] For a full discussion of the curious Thriae see S. Scheinberg, 'The bee maidens of the Homeric *Hymn to Hermes*', *HSCP* 83 (1979), pp.1-28.

[21] Cf. W. Burkert, 'Kekropidensage und Arrheporia', *Hermes* 94 (1966), pp.1-25.

indispensable element for growth among all living things. The goddesses appear as creatures who both shed light on and give brilliance to those whom they favour, and their radiance is a gift to victor and poet both. The laudator illuminates his laudandus and his city with his song (*O.* 9.21-2), and the subject himself becomes a source of the far-shining light of fame (*N.* 3.64). Song appears in the form of a torch or beacon (*I.* 3/4.61), and the victor blazes with the light of the Graces (*P.* 5.45). One of the Graces herself bears the name of Aglaia, an expression of the radiance she bestows (*O.* 14.13). Light stands as a foil to the darkness which is the very negation of forces of growth and the poet's powers. Light represents the two cardinal properties of poetry, memory and truth, which counter the darkness which comes when men are forgotten through want of celebration in song. The Muses, nine daughters of Mnemosyne, are the ones who 'love to remember' (*N.* 1.12), and enable poets to conquer the transience of mortal glory and fame. They also guarantee the truth of his words, instructing Hesiod at *Theogony* 25, and the Muses and Alatheia together defeat the dark power of lies and blame at *O.* 10.3f. They are the sources of the light and water which Pindar brings to his laudandus:

> σκοτεινὸν ἀπέχων ψόγον,
> ὕδατος ὥτε ῥοὰς φίλον ἐς ἄνδρ' ἄγων
> κλέος ἐτήτυμον αἰνέσω·

(N. 7.61-3)

Keeping off dark reproach, as though by bearing streams of water to the man I esteem, I shall praise true glory.

The varied images of light and water and the Muses come together in the extended metaphor at *N.* 7.11f., where Pindar describes the complex relationship between poetry and the achievement it celebrates. Here, by virtue of the Muses and of Memory, the poet overcomes darkness and holds up a mirror to the deed the ode recalls. The symbol of the mirror's polished surface evokes the water which reflects back an image, and sends out light from its face. Possessed of the forces of illumination, growth and nurture, poetry moves with its own impetus and enjoys an independent life. Once articulated, it is an autonomous thing, capable of future growth and self-renewal, unquenchable in the rays which it sends out through time and space.[22] It not only participates in the natural life processes going on about it, but has the capacity to sustain motion in other things, assuming the fostering powers of the goddesses who presided over its own origins and those of the man who first gave it expression.

As a flourishing force, poetry extends from the natural environment into the city realm. Again, the Muses, Nymphs and Graces participate in its journey and have an integral part in the reception of the athlete and his celebration in song. Nymphs leave their waters, trees and meadows and appear in the form of city founders. Rhodes, as *Olympian* 7 relates, was once a Nymph who married with the sun's rays in the establishment of the island which bears her name. Cyrene, raised in the mountains and forests of northern Greece, comes southward to Africa where she inhabits the 'fair, flourishing third root of the continent' (*P.* 9.8). Like other goddesses, the Nymphs of the city or shrine in which they dwell continue to possess and to promote life, and are often the very source of the fertility of their land. Like the Muses and Graces, their role with regard to the victorious athlete, son of their soil, is one of welcome, integrating him back into his native city. Pindar traces the connections between the city Nymph, the athlete and the poet's song; the ode and goddess exist in close communion; in invoking the Nymph, the poem rouses her attention and invites her to look with particular favour on the individual whom it celebrates. The poet must bestow lavish praise upon the city in order to make the Nymph kindly disposed and willing to lend her sacred presence to the welcoming ceremony (*P.* 2.1-8; *P.* 12.1-5; *N*, 1.1-18). In *P.* 9.71-2 the victor actually bestows the flowers he has won upon the city Nymph as she welcomes him home, and the garlands with which the athlete is honoured become the tangible manifestations of the fertility of the goddess in whose presence the crowning ceremony is re-enacted. The festivities which include the performance of the song are the visible signs of abundance, and occur under the particular patronage of the Graces.[23] Blossom

---

[22] On the character of poetry as an autonomous life force see M. Detienne, *Les Maîtres de vérité dans la Grèce archaïque* (Paris, 1967), pp.53-5.

[23] H. Gundert, in *Pindar und sein Dichterberuf* (Frankfurt, 1935), stresses the role of Charis as a link between the deed of the individual and the community to which he returns. For the role of Nymphs in the city see Mullen, op.cit., p.79f.

and celebration are jointly expressed in the name of Thalia, the goddess who takes her place alongside her sisters Aglaia and Euphrosyne in combining natural luxuriance with communal rejoicing.

Within the city realm, the poem takes on a broader scope, uniting elements of music, song, and dance with the general revelry which it stirs up. These are the perennial pastimes of the goddesses whom Pindar invokes as helpers in his poetic task, and their presence lends the essential quality of permanence to the momentary events. In participating in the celebration of the mortal victor on earth, the Muses and Graces continue the role they play among the immortal gods and, through their metaphoric attendance, Pindar suggests how the subject of his ode may share in the undying glory which the Olympians enjoy. The tradition of the goddesses who sing and dance is a very ancient one; the immortal *choreia* appears in the *Homeric Hymn* 26.9 and again at 27.15 where Artemis arrives with a chorus of the Muses and Graces in attendance. Pan is likewise accompanied by Nymphs who hymn his birth and deeds and dance in celebration of the god (19.19). The present-day *kômos* which enacts and sings the glory of the deeds of men, and invokes the heroes and gods who participate in their achievement, carries with it the suggestion of the ever-dancing Muses and Graces. At *P.* 1.1-4, Pindar intimates parity between the mortal perform-ance which is about to begin before the assembled audience and the divine celebration on Mount Olympus where music preserves an eternal harmony. He establishes a close parallel between the living *kômos* and the figurative band of the Muses in *N.* 5.23f., when he points out that the tale of Peleus and the grace he received from Zeus is not only the subject of the poet's verse, but of the song which the Muses themselves perform. While Pindar praises his mortal athlete, the Muses proclaim their hero who triumphed in a wrestling match, and sing their epinician before the presence of Zeus himself. The Muses and the Graces sometimes even sing in mortal company; at *P.* 3.89f. they appear at the marriage of Peleus and Thetis among the other gods who join in feasting with the mortals. The Graces are the source of all dance and feasting among the Olympians where a state of permanent revelry exists (*O.* 14.8-9).

Each act of celebration among men recalls the behaviour of the immortal gods, and Pindar establishes the analogy by placing his goddesses at the heart of the festivities which victory promotes. His poems contain numerous symposial motifs which permit him to mingle the goddesses with their earthly counterparts. The poet invokes the Muses at the opening of *I.* 6 where men mix together a bowl of the goddesses' verse and the wine bowl itself may carry the Muse within it, a source of inspiration and 'sweet prophet of song' (*N.* 9.50). The drink from which the poet draws his power becomes the wine that crowns the festal celebration as men gather together in general rejoicing, dining and drinking. Feasting is the communal activity par excellence where men forget their differences and where the athlete may be assured of a gracious reception back into his native city. The goddesses thus attend the poem and its celebrants at every step of the way, from the first moment of the ode's conception in their gardens and woodland haunts to its delivery in the city. They are present in the festal procession which brings the athlete and poet to the place of the song's performance and at the feast where poetry is also sung and where the garlanded participants celebrate the victor's achievement. When, at the opening of *N.* 9 Pindar declares 'I shall dance in a *kômos*, Muses, from Sicyon to Aetna', he invites the goddesses to attend the poet and his chorus throughout the long course of events which epinicia involve.

The goddesses do not only give a smooth passage to the individual ode in its particular composition and performance. They also symbolise the poem's capacity for infinite renewal and repetition whenever men who dance and sing summon the goddesses to their presence. They are concerned with the two aspects of song which grant it an immortal life, with its beauty and its durability. Muses and Graces stand as twin facets of the song; while images of fertility, soil, light, wind and water are common to both, recalling their common origins in chthonic cult, Pindar differentiates between them in his choice of metaphors;[24] he reserves images of flowers and of blossoms for the Graces alone (*O.* 2.50; *O.* 7.11; *N.* 5.54), evoking the transient beauty of growing things and the sudden loveliness which charms men into forgetfulness of their mortal condition. To the Muses is owed the staying powers of the song which everlastingly recalls past deeds. They associate with such firm objects as chariots, ships, bows and arrows, bowls, stones, staffs and gold. In plaiting the great

[24] Ibid. p.83f.

wreath of song, they mingle metal with the coral of the sea, creating the supreme model for the transient crown of leaves the victor receives from the hands of the Graces (*N.* 7.77-9). Brilliant blossoms and fixity also belong to the ode that received performance; though the actual dance and song are but a momentary act, delivered by a band of mortal celebrants, the eternally revelling Muses and Graces stand as guarantors of the possibility of repetition and renewed performance.

5

Craftsmanship

Poetry has so far been seen as a product of Nature and of the forces which inhabit it. In a fertile setting, the poet composes his verse and finds in the flowers and plants about him symbols for creativity and for song. He looks to the inhabitants of his poetic haunts, the Muses and Graces, for inspiration and, by virtue of their patronage, claims a status that is semi-divine. He is an *aoidos*, a bard to the Homeric sense who speaks through the agency of his immortal patrons, and belongs to an ancient tradition which makes poetry a divine gift, originally the possession of the gods and later practised by their children on earth. Through metaphor, Pindar adds another facet to his representation of his task, a further element in the interplay between transience and permanence which his symbols describe. The singer is also a *poiêtês*, a fabricant. He no longer looks to the Muses to furnish him with the material of his verse, but creates songs which stand as autonomous feats of personal art and technique. As the practitioner of this trade, Pindar draws on the craftsman's realm for metaphors of composition and song. His *technê* or skill sets him among the *dêmiourgoi*, the category of skilled workers which once included brotherhoods of diviners, heralds, healers and bards as well as artisans who fashioned metal, stone, wood and cloth. The epinician poet is a paid craftsman who must deliver an artefact according to his patron's specifications. The song as craft adds a new dimension to its many-sided nature; images of workmanship contribute to its durability, making it a lasting testimonial to the laudator and laudandus. The 'crafted' nature of the song, however, admits the possibility of illusion, counterfeit and change. It is only through the union of the realms of craftsmanship and nature that the ode may stand as a symbol both of everlasting beauty and of truth, when the poet-fabricant combines skill with inspiration.

Both song and craftsmanship are concerned with harmony, the

concordant assembly of diverse elements so as to admit neither gap nor fissure. The language of music and carpentry coincide, carrying an association which the Greeks acknowledged from an early time. The verb *ararisko*, fit together, lies at the root of *harmonia*, a term which once described a joint such as a mason or a carpenter would use and which later came to signify the chords of a lyre.[1] The carpenter is son to the joiner in Homer's representation of Tekton Harmonides (*Il.* 5.59), and the notion of fitting together extends from carpentry to music in the frequent metaphor of the poet-carpenter. Both in the *Homeric Hymn* (3.164) and Pindar's *P.* 3.113-14, singers are craftsmen who fasten their songs together.

The metaphor of harmony as fixing together enters the epinician ode at many levels. It describes the literal union Pindar must create between the music, words and dance, and takes on a concrete realisation when the performers join hands in the chorus. At the more figurative level, the poet must match the subject to the word and theme, and build a tight joint between the laudandus and the particular song Pindar has composed in his honour. The poet uses the term *enarmoxai*, to be fitted, to describe the joining of athlete and verse (*I.* 1.16), while the metaphor of the sandal that fits the foot designates the close match between the subject and the song, the aptness of the one for the other (*O.* 6.8). *O.* 3 opens with an extended image of yoking and joining, a natural extension of the context of horsemanship which the poem celebrates; Pindar enjoys the help of the Muses as he fits the voice of the revellers to the Dorian metre (4-6) while he himself stands with his head 'yoked about' with crowns (6-7), a symbol for the duty of praise he must fulfil.[2] He then passes to the blending of the lyre, flute and verse, using a compound of one of his favourite terms *mignumi*, mix, to represent the harmonious whole (8-9). Mixing and matching may be seen as an image for the entire task on which the poet has embarked; he is concerned with comparing one element of the occasion to another, with setting the song and the victory it celebrates in relation to every other feature of the event. Like the

[1] Cf. P. Chantraine, *Dictionnaire étymologique de la langue grecque* (Paris, 1974) for the development of the term. A long-established Indo-European tradition links the activity of the poet to that of artisans like carpenters.

[2] Binding and yoking traditionally represent the duty a man must fulfil. See Onians, op.cit., p.407, n.1.

craftsman, he draws his materials from various areas, and fixes all together in the creation of a new composite. Metaphor is naturally a major device of his trade.

The processes of assembly and working together apply to all the crafts which Pindar selects for his metaphors of poetic composition and for the finished product, verse. Some are traditional images which have long associated craft with speech and poetry. The weaving of speech already appears in Homer at *Il.* 3.212, and so frequent is the figurative use of this activity that the verb *huphainô* virtually comes to signify create.[3] This particular craft has close links with Pindar's practice and his themes; it serves as an image of the poet's satisfaction of the requirement of his art when he creates a tightly woven cloth, compact but including all relevant material:[4]

καιρὸν εἰ φθέγξαιο, πολλῶν πείρατα συντανύσαις
ἐν βραχεῖ, μείων ἕπεται μῶμος ἀνθρώ-
πων·

(*P.* 1.81-2)

If I speak appropriately, drawing together the strands of all things concisely, less blame will follow on from men.

Like the weaver, Pindar produces material in which he covers his laudandus and his metaphors of song portray the poet wrapping verse about his subject, enfolding him in the cloth of praise (*I.* 1.33).[5] The dancers themselves perform intricate weaving patterns with their bodies and feet, and poet and chorus' activity evoke the actual plaited crown which the triumphant athlete receives. While weaving involves the combination of warp and woof, the metal worker forges together his different substances. The metaphor applies to the fabrication of song when Pindar describes the Muse at *N.* 7.77-9, who does not weave but welds together her garland of song:

[3] Silk denies that the term *huphainô* applied to song is a poetic cliché. For his evidence see p.181, n.11.
[4] For discussion of this particular metaphor see Onians, op.cit., p.338. Dionysus of Halicarnassus will later compare a poem to a precious cloth which the hand of the poet creates, bringing together the different kinds of speech it involves. See *On the Style of Demosthenes* 8.
[5] Gerber concludes that the image at *O.* 1.8 is not a clothing metaphor. Gerber, op.cit., p.27.

Μοῖσά τοι
κολλᾷ χρῦσόν ἔν τε λευκὸν ἐλέφανθ᾿ ἁμᾶ
καὶ λείριον ἄνθεμον ποντίας ὑφελοῖσ᾿ ἐέρσας.

The Muse forges together gold and white ivory with the lily
flower, taking it up from the sea's dew.

Men's words as well as their songs are fastened together and
Pindar bids Hieron forge his tongue against the anvil of justice
(*P.* 1.86). Another individual who sets together different shapes,
forms and substances is the builder who places stone upon stone
in constructing the homes, palaces and temples that appear in
Pindar's verse. The poet-architect metaphor is a highly
traditional one which Pindar applies to his particular manner of
proceeding in the composition of song.[6] He equates the opening
of the ode, its prelude, with the building's foundations since both
are the base on which the final edifice must rest (*P.* 7.3). The
building blocks which the poem sets down serve as foundation
stones both for the particular song he writes and for the men who
will create subsequent structures. Pindar's most extended
metaphor of building appears at *O.* 6.1-4, where the poet traces
the progress of his temple song:

Χρυσέας ὑποστάσαντες εὐ-
τειχεῖ προθύρῳ θαλάμου
κίονας ὡς ὅτε θαητὸν μέγαρον
πάξομεν· ἀρχομένου δ᾿ ἔργου πρόσωπον
χρὴ θέμεν τηλαυγές.

Setting golden pillars beneath the well-walled portal of the
chamber, let us build as we would a wonderul palace; for
it is necessary to give to the beginning of a work a shining
facade.

The monuments of words which the poet establishes serve as
permanent reminders of the worth of the man in whose honour
they are constructed, a fitting image for the undying existence
which the song itself promotes (*N.* 8.46-8). The crafts which the
poet practises frequently involve the presence of the Muses who

---

[6] Cf. J. Taillardat, *Les Images d'Aristophane* (Paris, 1965), p.438.

themselves work in durable materials. They stand by the poet as he discovers the *neosigalon tropon*, new-shining measure, with which he fixes his song together (*O.* 3.4), and concern themselves, like their protégé, with the harmony of the world in which they dwell, presiding over an equitable balance in the cosmos (*P.* 1.10-12).

Harmony, the co-existence of varied elements in a cohesive whole, is the concern of the doctor as well as the worker in inanimate stuff. The human organism, like the natural environment, must be well balanced; the body according to Greek medical theory is made up of four humours in exact proportions to one another, blood, phlegm, yellow and black bile. Disease occurs when one exceeds another, or when the elements became unmixed, disturbing the *isonomia* or balance that Alcmaeon of Croton described as health.[7] The doctor is a craftsman, practitioner of a *technê* that involves surgical operations and skill of hand, as well as diagnosis and the administering of drugs. Pindar establishes a close link between healing, craftsmanship and song; Asclepius is a *tektón* or carpenter who sets upright men's limbs (*P.* 3.6), the poet the craftsman who sets his song straight (*O.* 3.3; *O.* 7.21). The figures of doctor and poet hold many similarities: both are itinerant individuals whose task it is to provide antidotes to pain. Song is a *pharmakon*, a medicine, that heals, and Pindar terms the revelry of which it is a part the best of doctors (*N.* 4.1). In making men forget the pain they have endured, the ode acts as more than a drug; it is a charm such as a magician might use. Healing, song and magic once stood in close relation to one another, crafts all exhibited by Empedocles, the legendary doctor, poet and magician who cured men through magical incantation.[8] The use of drugs and incantation in combination was frequent practice in Ancient Egypt and in Greece, and Homer describes how the flow of blood from Odysseus' wound was staunched with a magical spell or *epaoidê* (*Od.* 19.457).[9] In

---

[7] For further discussion of balance as defining health see B. Fowler, 'Imagery of the *Prometheus Bound*', *AJPh* 78 (1957), pp.173-84, and G. Majno, *The Healing Hand; Man and Wound in the Ancient World* (Cambridge, Mass., 1975), pp.178-9.

[8] On the connections between magic, medicine and song see de Romilly, *Magic and Rhetoric*, op.cit., p.14f.

[9] Majno, op.cit., pp.125-8.

Pindar, Asclepius likewise heals with *malakais epaoidais*, soft spells (*P.* 3.51), and the potency of the spell that song could cast appears at *P.* 1.12 where it soothes even the minds of the gods. Poetry derives its power from the beauty of its words and music, and the *meligarues hymnoi*, melodious songs, which Pindar evokes at *P.* 3.64 cast a *philtron* or charm on men's souls. The Graces appear in Pindar as the embodiment of the charm that rests in song, leading a man into the abandonment of his rational sense (*O.* 1.30f.), and they fittingly are associated with Persuasion (Fr. 123.14). The diviner and the prophet are also magicians of a sort, interpreters of the divine will among men. They are likewise members of a professional band, also itinerant practitioners of their trade. Pindar frequently fuses his identity with that of the prophet (Fr. 52f.6), and he too makes predictions concerning the course of future events in the form of prayers and wishes for his laudandus' continuing good fortune.[10] A final member of this general group is the herald who traditionally enjoys a sacred status and acts as prophet in narrating events as yet unknown to his audience. Pindar serves as a herald in his proclamation of the athlete's triumph, announcing his name, ancestry and city to the assembled crowd. At *O.* 6.90-1 he addresses the chorus leader as an:

ἄγγελος ὀρθός,
ἠϋκόμων σκυτάλα Μοι-
σᾶν

upright messenger, a *skutalon* of the fair-haired Muses.

The *skutalon* was an intricate device designed by the Spartans for sending secret dispatches, intelligible only to those who understood its mechanism.

Some of the artefacts which Pindar includes in his metaphors of craft require as much skill in the handling as the making, and he draws not merely on the technicians but also on those who use the product of the craftsman's labour. These men stand in the same relation to their instrument as the poet to his material and

---

[10] The affinities between poet and prophet are discussed by F.M. Cornford, *Principium Sapientiae: a study of the origins of Greek philosophical thought* (Cambridge, 1952), p.80f.

the requirements of his genre. The chariot and the ship not only represent the high point of the craftsman's art but also make demands on the knowledge of the driver and helmsman who direct their course. Greek thinking drew many affinities between the ship and horse or chariot, the rigging and the harness, the navigator and the charioteer.[11] At *P.* 4.24-5, Pindar refers to the bit and bridle of the vessel Argo, and opens *I.* 5 with a celebration of the goddess Theia who directs the motion of both ship and horse (4-6). Both have many applications to the ode in a literal and figurative capacity; the chariot was the actual vessel in which the laudandus might achieve his triumph, the ship the craft that would bring him to the site of the Games, and take the poet to his distant court. The ship at sea is not unlike the chariot on the track; both the field of athletics where the race was held and the open sea have their points of special danger, critical moments and sudden reversals.[12] Those who seek to travel safely must observe the nature of their element, and the laws of their craft. Numerous analogies suggest themselves between athletics, navigation and the composition of song. Both trainer and poet serve as helmsman, as one guides the athlete to his victory (*I.* 3/4.89b), and the other delivers moral strictures concerning the correct course a man's life should follow. The chariot and the ship are Pindar's two favourite poetic vehicles in which he accomplishes his journey of song. Like the navigator and charioteer, he adapts to the changing conditions, respecting the demands his genre makes. He must let out the sail at the appropriate moment, giving full vent to his praise, or bring it in again in order to alter his course (*N.* 5.50f.). He rouses up his horses at the beginning of his journey, but turns them on to a briefer road when time runs short (*P.* 4.247-8). Poet, sailor and driver are all concerned with *kairos*, the propitious moment which a man must seize and which gives him an opportunity to exercise his skill. The time span which the craftsman knows is very different from normal chronology; within the framework of the technical operation time moves rapidly, ever changing, and contains but one brief moment when an opportunity may be

---

[11] Cf. M. Detienne, 'The sea crow', in R.L. Gordon (ed.) *Myth, Religion and society* (Cambridge, 1981), p.29 and T.C.W. Stinton, 'The riddle at Colonus', *GRBS* 17 (1976), p.323f.

[12] Detienne, ibid. p.23f.

grasped, that point where human action coincides with the natural process of motion and development. The poet too must catch this instant, bringing his own skill into the victor's moment of glory.[13]

While the craftsman's activity suggests poetic composition, the products of his labour display the same properties as the Pindaric song. The poet makes metaphor of those objects which possess particular value, often one quite independent of their monetary worth,[14] and draws on their mythical and religious associations in portraying the quasi-divinity of his song. The chariot is the poetic vehicle par excellence, and also the embodiment of song itself. It is the possession of the gods and, in Pindar, belongs particularly to the Muses by virtue of their divine status and role in poetry.[15] It is the symbol of aristocratic wealth and privilege and distinguishes the social class for whom Pindar wrote his songs. Another symbol for the ode is the *thêsauros* (*P.* 6.7/8), no ordinary home but originally the place where jewels and clothes of value were kept. It later came to serve as an offertory box, the container for cult objects.[16] Bowls also carry verse, which assumes the sacral character of the libations which were poured from the precious vessels. At *I.* 6.1-3, the bowl has a poetic, athletic and religious significance, evoking the triple libation which traditionally honoured Zeus:

Θάλλοντος ἀνδρῶν ὡς ὅτε συμποσίου
δεύτερον κρατῆρα Μοισαίων μελέων
κίρναμεν Λάμπωνος εὐαέθλου γενεᾶς ὕπερ

Just like men when the feast is at its height, so we mix together a second bowl of the Muses' melodies in honour of Lampon's race of fine athletes.

Another religious offering was the robe, and Hecabe chooses one

---

[13] On the role of *kairos* in the craftsman's task see J.-P. Vernant, *Mythe et pensée chez les Grecs* (Paris, 1965), p.242.

[14] Objects which carry an inherent value are discussed in L. Gernet, 'La notion mythique de la valeur en Grèce', in *Anthropologie de la Grèce antique* (Paris, 1968), pp.93-137.

[15] M. Simpson, 'The chariot and the bow as metaphors for poetry in Pindar's odes', *TAPA* 100 (1969), pp.437-73.

[16] Gernet, op.cit., p.129.

with magnificent workmanship to serve as a gift to Athena at
Il. 6.294. Pindar's woven stuffs share the status of *agalmata*, a
term which carries notions of both adornment and worship. All
such metaphors point to the sacral nature of the epinician ode,
an integral part, Pindar suggests, of the Games which are
themselves religious festivals. These cyclical events com-
memorate the contests once held around the tomb of the dead
hero, and celebrate the gods in whose particular honour they
were established. The song serves as an offering to the divine
patrons, and to the dead who continue to preside over the Games
from the hero shrines in which they dwell.[17]

Further descriptions highlight the precious nature of the song.
A highly worked object naturally possesses more value than a
plain and simple one, and the terms *poikilos*, many-coloured,
and *daidalos*, cunningly wrought, express the intricate techniques involved.[18] The verb *poikillô* originally described
embroidery, the ornamentation of cloth, but came to be used of
anything variegated or made up of many different elements.
Twice Pindar describes his songs as *poikiloi* (*O.* 6.87; *N.* 5.42),
emphasising both the quality of the craftsmanship and the
variety of notes, metres and steps which went into the completed
ode. The term appears in his metaphor of the Lydian mitre,
kanachêda pepoikilmenan, embroidered with ringing sound
(*N.* 8.15), and is combined with an image of weaving at
O. 6.86-7. *Poikilos* may refer to many things, animate and still,
but *daidalos* is reserved for products of divine and human
craftsmanship. The latter quality bridges the realms of art and
manufacture, and suits the Pindaric song which portrays itself as
a combination of the two. The term is used of polished surfaces,
of jewelry, of embroidered cloth or wood and metal inlay. Pindar
uses it in a literal capacity at *P.* 5.36 where it describes the
victor's harness, and in a metaphoric sense at *O.* 1.105 where it
indicates the poet's creation of his song. It evokes all the
embellishment and adornment which makes the Pindaric ode a
thing of remarkable beauty and craftsmanship.

The highly worked nature of the song points the way towards

---

[17] Mullen, op.cit., p.75.
[18] For a full account of the meaning and application of the two terms see F.
Frontisi-Ducroux, *Dédale: mythologie de l'artisan en Grèce ancienne* (Paris,
1975).

the possibility of counterfeit or deceit which the poet's activity may involve.[19] Pindar uses the craft metaphor as a means of establishing the contrasting poles of truth and falsehood, of genuine skill and imitation on which his own claim for the truth and beauty of his account rests. His treatment of the theme of craft and skill may be seen within the broader context of the social climate of his age, and the ambiguous status which the craftsman and his trade held within the city.[20] Society's attitude towards craft changed as the skills and artefacts of the tradesman became divorced from their magical and religious associations. Once *technê* was revered, an integral part of sacred rites, and a gift which the gods granted to men. The *Iliad* and the *Odyssey* involve Athena and Hephaistos with the craftsman's activity and describe Odysseus' painstaking construction of his bed and raft without any suggestion that the task might be unworthy of him. Indeed, he is the master craftsman celebrated with the term *polumêtis*, of many skills. However, while one view equated the acquisition of technology with cultural progress, the means by which men might achieve a civilised existence, another saw it as symptomatic of decline, a departure from a former happy state when men lived from natural produce alone. It represents man's divorce from nature, not his participation in its forces and gifts. This double approach is reflected in the character of Prometheus, cultural benefactor to man and the cause of his rupture with the gods. In attempting to grant to men divine attributes, he angers the immortals and leaves mortals skilled in craft but abandoned by the gods.[21] The nature of poetry itself changed alongside that of craft; it also underwent a

---

[19] The truth/falsehood dichotomy which the poet's art involved became increasingly important as rhetoric influenced approaches to literature. Discussions may be found in Detienne, *Les Maîtres de vérité*, op.cit., P. Pucci, *Hesiod and the Language of Poetry* (Baltimore, London, 1971); the final chapter of C. Ramnoux, *Héraclite ou l'homme entre les choses et les mots* (Paris, 1959); and C.P. Segal, 'Gorgias and the psychology of the Logos', *HSCP* 66 (1962), pp.95-155. For Pindar's own approach, K. Svoboda, 'Les idées de Pindare sur la poésie', *Aegyptus* 32 (1952), pp.108-20.

[20] A. Burford, *Craftsmen in Greek and Roman Society* (London, 1972), p.185f. For further material on the craftsman's status see A. Aymard, 'Hiérarchie du travail et autarcie individuelle dans la grèce archaïque', in *Etudes d'histoire ancienne* (Paris, 1967), p.329f.

[21] The two faces of the Prometheus myth may, in fact, be derived from two separate sources. Cf. L. Séchan, *Le Mythe de Prométhée* (Paris, 1951), p.13f.

process of secularisation in the fifth and fourth centuries when, under the influence of rhetoric, technique rather than divine inspiration became the focus of attention.[22] The poet lost his semi-sacral status as spokesman of the gods, and poetry became a profession, based on commission and payment. Pindar regrets the poet's entry into the world of commerce and recalls the days when:

ἁ Μοῖσα γὰρ οὐ φιλοκερδής
πω τότ᾽ ἦν οὐδ᾽ ἐργάτις·

(*I.* 2.6)

the Muse was never greedy for gain, nor did she work for hire.

Pindar evokes the double nature of craft in establishing the negative foil to his own practice of his art. He draws on the same vocabulary from the artisan's realm to describe both the beautiful and guileful nature of song, suggesting that it is the very loveliness of the poet's speech that enchants men into forfeiting the truth and accepting a lying account. The single figure, Grace, acts as a source of both charm and falsehood:

Χάρις δ᾽, ἅπερ ἅπαντα τεύχει τὰ μείλιχα θνατοῖς,
ἐπιφέροισα τιμὰν καὶ ἄπιστον ἐμήσατο πιστόν
ἔμμεναι τὸ πολλάκις·

(*O.* 1.30-2)

Grace, who fashions everything that is sweet for mortals, brings honour and often makes that which is incredible credible.

Men are led astray by tales *dedaidalmenoi pseudesi poikilois*, embellished with many-coloured lies (*O.* 1.29), representations of the tricks and traps which craftsmanship may hide beneath its surface. The terms *poikilos* and *daidalos* express the changing,

---

[22] Detienne, op.cit. details four elements in the secularisation of poetry: the practice of poetry as a profession, the definition of the poetic work as a work of illusion, the devaluation of memory from a religious to a secular skill and the rejection of Alatheia as the cardinal attribute of poetry; p.106f. See also Ramnoux, op.cit.

shifting appearance which the play of materials creates, and they are the devices of Metis who personifies flux and metamorphosis.[23] Metaphors of craft traditionally describe attempts to trick and deceive. Men weave together their plots and Pindar speaks of Hippolyte who pieces together a lying, fabricated tale (*N*. 5.29) in her desire to deceive her husband. Tinting and dyeing are another means of hiding the essence of an object, and at *O*. 4.17 Pindar must give the assurance that he has not coloured his tale with a lie.

Attempts to disguise the true nature of an object or deed are the marks of false skill, contrasting with the genuine technique and talent which Pindar represents. Pindar's handling of the topos of the poet's skill is a complex one, describing both a valuable attribute, the *sophia* which comes as the bequest of the Muses, and the means by which counterfeiters can lay claim to the true poet's status. He distinguishes between talent that is innate, or comes from a divine source, and that which men merely learn or acquire through imitation (*O*. 2.86f.; *N*. 3.40f.). The master poet speaks according to his nature, his *phua*, the lesser man is a mere pupil or mimic. In every case *to de phuai kratiston*, what comes from a man's inner nature is best (*O*. 9.100).[24] Socrates will later develop this idea of true skills and false, dividing those which are based on knowledge, rule and truth from those that are mere *empeiria*, gained from trial and error. The philosopher places medicine in the first category, the true skill the poet doctor practises, and rhetoric in the second (*Gorgias* 426b, 464f.).

For the philosopher concerned with notions of the real, the craftsman's activity had little or no relevance, a mere imitation of reality, an *eidôlon* based on the mirroring of truth. Indeed, the artefact was worse than imitation since it created an impression of life which had no correspondence to the external object. Achilles' shield is so skilfully forged by Hephaistos that its scenes appear to possess a life of their own (*Il*. 18.548-9). The word likewise can assume an independent existence, one which may lead men into false beliefs through the charm and sweetness it

[23] For a full discussion of the nature of Metis see M. Detienne et J.-P. Vernant, *Les Ruses de l'intelligence: la métis des Grecs* (Paris, 1974).

[24] For further treatment of the nature of the poet see C.M. Bowra, *Pindar* (Oxford, 1964), p.1f. and Nisbet and Hubbard, op.cit., on *Odes* 1.1.29.

conveys. The poet is no longer merely the mouthpiece for the divine, the agent through whom oracles and sacred legend are preserved, but an autonomous creator in himself, dangerous counterpart to the gods. Pindar constructs the rival poet, the false practitioner of *technê*, the lying tale in order to cancel them out with his portrayal of the singer as participant in the life of nature. Poet and craftsman both may remain within the natural context, and authentic craftsmanship involves the realisation of the *phusis* of an object. The artist must have an understanding of the primacy of natural forms, and seek to make them tangible and visible within the artefacts he creates.[25] The song as craft does not attempt to transform nature, but to represent and re-enact events both of the distant and the immediate past. Pindar tends towards the most accurate account possible of the victory and triumph through the medium of words, music and dance. In making of the particular victory an idealised, representative event, he does not change its character, but simply realises what is latent in the deed itself.

The metaphor of craft adds a novel dimension to Pindar's representation of song as the simultaneous incarnation of life and permanence. Unlike the images previously looked at, the metaphor draws on the inanimate realm, casting song not as something that lives, moves and grows but as a fixed object, immutable. In its firm form, the song as artefact gives expression to the way in which Pindar takes the life and motion of the athlete and sets it in lasting material. The poet indicates his own powers when twice the image of the *stêlê*, gravestone, follows on immediately after a dead man's name, a symbol of the victory over death that song achieves (*N.* 4.80-1; *N.* 8.44-8).[26] Sometimes Pindar places his metaphors of craft in complementary relation to his images of flowers and wreaths, juxtaposing the two sides of his art. He may also contrast his poetic products with the forces of flux and change which seek to disturb their stable structure. The treasure house of songs stands unaltered by the buffeting winds and rains, as enduring as the ceaseless onslaught of the elements (*P.* 6.10-14). Pindar's emphasis on his skill as part of nature prevents a divorce between *phusis* and *poiêsis*, and preserves the poet's art as a true representation of reality,

[25] Cf. Vernant, *Mythe et pensée*, op.cit., p.233f.
[26] Mullen, op.cit., p.73.

untouched by artifice. The products he creates are the joint possessions of gods and men, and the Muses and Graces involve themselves closely with his craftsmanship. If the Pindaric song is to last for all eternity, it must be the accurate account of the events it celebrates, and Pindar's metaphors of craft assure the patron that the goods that he receives will satisfy the demands of time, truth and loveliness.

6

The Winds and Waves

Pindar's odes derive their ability to span two conditions, two times, two levels of meaning from their status as moving objects, and a major set of the poet's metaphors are concerned with mobility and passage. This is, in part, a development of the theme already discussed which made of the poem a living, moving object capable of promoting growth in those it celebrated. The symbols of motion and of travel emphasise the instability of human life and fortunes, introducing metaphors of vicissitude and change throughout the poem's course. This constantly shifting backdrop serves Pindar's encomiastic ends, creating a dark foil for the triumph of the victor which the song will cast in lasting form. Motion, impermanence and change all come together in the image of the voyage which functions at every level of the ode's subject and theme, binding song and material into a close complex. The voyage describes the lives of the individual athlete and poet, that of the chorus and the audience who stand as representatives of the broader interests which Pindar must address. The poem as well as its subject is a travelling thing, embarked on its own voyage of changing language, theme and structure. Pindar chooses metaphors which both generate and reflect the movements of his verse and of the men it portrays; structure and imagery coincide as the changing sense of the words and the varying rhythm and metre reflect external motion in human fortunes at the individual and collective levels. The dancers likewise move in accordance with the patterns of strophe, antistrophe and epode, actual visualisations of the motion the poem describes. The vehicles which convey the theme of voyage lie within the experience of all men as the forces which animate their world; the seas and skies, winds, waves and clouds are the clearest symbols of ceaseless motion, transience and change. When combined with the song itself, they become representations of the ode's power to travel to the far corners of the earth, through space and time, and so to spread the glory of its patron.

Poets had long sought in the world of the external elements images of men's own desires, trials and emotions. The natural phenomena of sky and water lent themselves particularly well to metaphoric representation, permitting the poet to abstract from them the significance he required. Little understood, they were frequently given human shape and form, made minor deities or placed beneath the control of greater gods who dictated their shifting shape and behaviour. Pindar allows his maritime metaphors to emerge naturally from within the context of his odes and the experience of his audience. The ocean was a centre of concern for a nation which traded, fought and colonised by sea. It was a dominant feature in the life of both the poet and his subjects; Pindar composed his songs for men living all about the Mediterranean basin, some as far flung as Sicily and Africa, and the poet himself is known to have accomplished at least one sea voyage in fulfilment of his commission. Many of the city-states for whom he wrote were dependent on the sea, and the odes composed for citizens of Aegina contain a large amount of maritime imagery as suits their context. In turning from literal to figurative speech, Pindar draws on a long tradition of symbolic representations of this element.[1] In Homeric epic the sea is notoriously hostile, characterised as fishy, barren, black. The waves and the sea are the most frequent vehicles for descriptions of the violence and chaos of combat, representing the onslaught of dangerous forces outside a man's control. The ocean Pindar describes presents a constant threat to men, and the poet cautions against the wave that rolls up towards the ship (*N*. 6.55-7). Misfortune at sea serves as a metaphor for reversal of any kind, a shorthand for the complete destruction of a man or nation's fortunes, whether through personal disaster or through war. The image of the shipwrecked man describes Asopodorus at *I*. 1.36, and the stormy night at sea acts as a generalised portrait of all the hazards that attend a city (*O*. 6.100-1). The conflicts and reversals which the poet faces are also cast in maritime terminology as Pindar describes himself held fast about the waist

[1] Cf. A. Lesky, *Thalatta: Der Weg der Griechen zum Meer* (Vienna, 1947). Considerable information concerning the role of the sea in Pindar and other Greek poets and dramatists may be found in Péron, op.cit. on whom I draw throughout this chapter.

by the brine (*N*. 4.36-7). As a symbol for the forces which lie beyond human mastery, the sea includes the workings of such intangible devices as fate and fortune, time and destiny. It shares in the unpredictability these abstract influences display, making man a plaything at their mercy. At *O*. 12.5f., Pindar develops the image of men's fortunes embarked on a treacherous sea:

> αἱ γε μὲν ἀνδρῶν
> πόλλ᾽ ἄνω, τὰ δ᾽ αὖ κάτω
> ψεύδη μεταμώνια τάμνοισαι κυλίνδοντ᾽ ἐλπίδες·

The hopes of men are tossed, often up, and then down, as they cleave through vain illusions.

The metaphor expresses a major theme of this particular ode, the uncertainty of a man's destiny in the face of which the victor's achievement stands in greater glory.

The ceaseless motion of the seas and waves, their changing configuration, is in part a result of the wind and breezes that play across the watery surface. These too are shifting and unsure, also symbols of the instability of men's lives and of their necessary submission to greater forces which lie outside their understanding. Breezes appear repeatedly in Pindar's reminders of the ephemerality of all human happiness, and *O*. 7 closes with a sobering gnome:

> ἐν δὲ μιᾷ μοίρᾳ χρόνου
> ἄλλοτ᾽ ἀλλοῖαι διαιθύσσοισιν αὖραι.

(*O*. 7.94-5)

But in a single portion of time, different kinds of the breezes dart this way and that.

The unpredictable winds may bring a character good fortune or ill in random turn; the *ouros* is the favouring breeze which features at *O*. 13.28, but Pindaric winds may also be destructive, devastating the plant life which symbolises men's prosperity. Winds, like the waves, demand that we be flexible in our response, and the two elements combine in Pindaric metaphors of navigation where the individual as helmsman must alter the course of his ship or rearrange the rigging in accordance with the new direction the winds have assumed (*P*.4.291-3). The breath of the wind is not only external to man, but becomes more irresistible still when it appears in the shape of inner emotions which direct his behaviour towards happiness or misfortune. Pindar builds on the traditional representation of the *thumos*, or inner consciousness, as a breath which men inhale and expel.[2] It is a vaporous thing, sometimes visible. An outside wind may blow into a man, as in the case of Boreas who, breathing on him, revives Sarpedon, 'who had grievously breathed forth his *thumos*' (*Il.* 5.696f.). Disaster occurs when a man's internal breath is inconstant or uncertain, driving him along in contrary directions as do opposing breezes.[3] Success will never come to the individual who in Pindar's account:

> ψεφεννὸς ἀνὴρ
> ἄλλοτ᾽ ἄλλα πνέων οὔ ποτ᾽ ἀτ᾽ρεκεῖ
> κατέβα ποδί

(*N.* 3.41-3)

is a man in darkness, breathing this way and that and never achieves his goal with an unswerving foot.

The wind that is associated with emotion can shape a man's destiny no less than those which direct him from without. Winds and waves both represent the external influences which guide his course, and also the internal play of feeling and desire, just as random and compelling.

The ocean and the skies combine to determine the weather, and fair weather and foul symbolise the two possible states of a man's fortunes. The image of the calm day is again a traditional one, serving as a metaphor for prosperity and inner harmony.[4] Pindar holds up *eudia*, good weather, as the highest reward a man may achieve and characterises the human condition as one in which men can never know when they may enjoy fair weather to the end (*O.* 2.32-4). The constancy which calm skies signify belongs not to mortal realms, but to the idyllic lands inhabited

[2] Onians, op.cit., p.44f.
[3] Aeschylus, *Agamemnon* 187.
[4] E.g. Simonides 20 Diehl and further examples in Péron, op.cit., p.290f.

by the immortals and the favoured dead. Stormy conditions, when winds, skies and seas grow turbulent, are the antithesis of inner as well as external harmony, and represent emotion at its height; Cyrene battling against the wild beasts nevertheless possesses spirits which *phobôi d'ou kecheimantai*, are not storm-driven by fear. (*P.* 9.32). Bad weather is a familiar metaphor for war where the rain shower represents the spilling of blood (*I.* 5.49-50) and the *phonon nephelê*, cloud of slaughter, at *N.* 9.37-38 conveys the irresistible approach of carnage which battle involves. Calm and storm act in partnership, one following closely upon the other. Like the winds and waves, the character of the weather lies quite outside man's mastery and he is reduced to invoking the aid of the gods who alone may calm the winds.[5] These rapid shifts serve as vehicles for Pindar's portrayal of the constant heights and depths in men's condition, and appear in warnings against placing too much confidence in present prosperity. The changing fortunes of Pindar's subjects are thus cast against the broadest backdrop the poet can supply, and their trials are, in microcosm, reflections of the long-drawn-out conflicts in the natural world itself.

Faced with these shifting elements, each man embarks on his own particular voyage which takes him from birth to death, carried in the ship of his individual destiny.[6] Pindar uses the symbol of the ship or voyage of life to express certain recurrent themes, closely tied in with the effect of the changing force of the elements already discussed. On the maritime journey of life, man faces the uncertainty of his condition, the overwhelming influence of the gods, the necessity of danger and toil and the rapid shifts between rough and smooth passage which all human experience involves. Pindar further differentiates between the roles of the individuals embarked on this ship. Some may be pilots and helmsmen, others crew. The metaphor of the ship of state first appears in Archilochus, in Alcaeus and Theognis where the *kubernêtês*, helmsman, represents the aristocratic element in a city's constitution. The leader of the state appears in the now familiar guise of helmsman at *P.* 1.86, and again at

---

[5] Cf. Nisbet and Hubbard, op.cit. ad Horace 1.12.31.

[6] Early representations of the person in the shape of a ship include Alcaeus 46 Diehl and Theognis 970b. In the *Prometheus Bound* Prometheus and Io are also portrayed as ships buffeted by the storm.

P. 10.72. The city accomplishes a voyage under the dictates not only of its leaders but also of the gods who are its founders and patrons. A maritime metaphor dominates the opening strophe of *O.* 12 where Pindar invokes *Tuchê*, the goddess Fortune, and celebrates her as the one through whom:

> ἐν πόντῳ κυβερνῶνται θοαί
> νᾶες, ἐν χέρσῳ τε λαιψηροὶ πόλεμοι
> κἀγοραὶ βουλαφόροι.

> (*O.* 12.3-5)

> swift-ships are steered at sea, rushing wars on the land and assemblies that bring forth counsels.

Men accomplish their voyage both at the individual and at the collective level, guided by internal whims and external directives, describing a direct or circuitous course.

Within the overall scheme of the ship of life and the play of the elements which it marks, Pindar focuses on two categories of men whose journeys possess a distinctive character. These are the poets and athletes whom his ode treats, individuals who embark on distant travels, whose ships carry them further than those of other men. Each victory is, in some sense, a voyage at whose close the triumphant athlete touches on the Pillars of Heracles, final symbol of the furthest reaches of human achievement (*N.* 3.21-2; *I.* 3/4.29-30). The victor and hero, more than other men, have a chance to master the forces which seek to mould their destinies, to harness them to their own designs. *O.* 12, through maritime imagery, introduces the powerful contrast between *Tuchê's* control of the world and man's inability to see what lies ahead for him. After focusing on human irrationality and weakness, Pindar introduces his victor whose career stands as a glorious example of the positive power of the incalculable, and the early emphasis on man's blindness and submission to illusion serves as a foil to the experience of Ergoteles.[7]

It is as a dark foil to the victory itself that the imagery of skies

---

[7] For a careful analysis of the role of *Tuchê* in this poem see F.J. Nisetich, 'The leaves of triumph and mortality: transformation of a traditional image in Pindar's *Olympian 12*', *TAPA* 107 (1977), pp.235-64.

and seas comes most prominently into play in Pindar's representation of his individual subject; success emerges with particular brilliance from the gloomy backdrop which Pindar designs, in which mortals must battle ceaselessly to overcome the forces ranged against them. Shifts in the winds and weather presage the resurgence of the individual's fortunes, and Arcesilus enjoys a sun-filled hearth after the storms of winter (*P.* 5.10-11). The poet uses the contrasting play of light and dark first to present Strepsiades, who appears lit up with the brilliance of the Muses, and then to show his ancestors in the midst of a bloody storm (*I.* 7.23f.). Pindar thus turns his metaphors towards his encomiastic ends, celebrating the man who may transcend the motion-filled condition in which he lives, and achieve one fixed moment of calm and sunshine. Victory, he suggests, is the one antidote to the vicissitudes and change of human existence; it is a good fortune which no wind or wave can move, a light whose rays cannot be extinguished.

It is the poet who can give lasting form to the moment of victory the athlete enjoys. Like his subject, he too rises above the turbulence which the winds and waves describe, and bends them to his will. The sea is of significance to the poet not merely as the medium through which he accomplishes his individual journey, but as a source of poetic inspiration, whose power he harnesses to his verse. Pindar draws on a traditional poetic conceit, that of speech as running water, and develops it further within his own complex of liquid symbols. The streams which Pindar evokes may belong either to the waters of the oceans or rivers; he describes fame mingled with 'streams of words' (*I.* 7.19) and, at *O.* 10.10, speaks of the tuneful wave, which washes away the pebble of his debt. The Muses gather up the coral from which they build their triple crown of song from the deep sea bed (*N.* 7.77-9). Sometimes the contrast between fresh inland water and the ocean brine serves Pindar's thematic ends; one is a sterile element, unable to sustain the living force of poetry, while the other possesses a regenerative power which nourishes plants, men and song.[8] In a *Partheneion*, Pindar seems to contrast the two, speaking first of drinking nectar and then avoiding brine

---

[8] Cf. C.P. Segal, 'Pindar's *7th Nemean*', *TAPA* 98 (1967), pp.431-80. The emphasis the author places on the contrast between the salt water of the sea and the refreshing inland waters is perhaps excessive.

(Fr. 94b.76-8).

Winds and waves combine in some of Pindar's descriptions of inspiration, and the poet portrays himself overcome by the *kallirhoaisi pnoais*, fair-flowing breezes (*O*. 6.83). Inspiration may be literally blown into the poet as in the case of Hesiod whose Muses *enepneusan de moi audên/thespin*, breathed into me an inspired voice (*Theogony* 31-2). The Muse's breath is traditionally a sweet one, presaging the quality of the poet's song (*O*. 13.22). Metaphors of winds and waves express the notion of poetic creativity as a force which the individual draws in and then sends out in delivering his song to men. The song assumes the same shape and form of the elements which first inspired it; Pindar is the source of the waters from which his laudandus drinks, which satisfies his thirst and causes his fame to grow. His is the breath which guides his patrons on a favourable course, a strong breeze that may carry them on towards future victory and success. The coincidence of imagery between the victor and the poet reinforces the close link between the two, as both continue their journeys beneath the influence of the Muses' waters and breath.

The forces of inspiration readily match the symbol of the vessel in which Pindar carries out his particular journey. He travels both at the literal and figurative levels, embarking for the court of Hieron where he must deliver his ode (*P*. 3.68), and marking a course which should serve as an example and admonition to the victor whom he celebrates (*I*. 7.40f.). More particularly, his vessel is the ship of song which traces its voyage from the poem's opening to its close (e.g. *P*. 11.39; *N*. 3.26-7; *O*. 13.49). Through his metaphors of maritime travel, Pindar addresses the theme of poetic composition, and of the poet's relation to the material at hand. He is responsible for the navigation of his ship, and his careful handling represents his satisfaction of the demands of his genre. The theme of appropriateness appears in the image of the poet raising and lowering his sails, catching the full blast of the inspiring winds when praise should reach its height, letting down the sheet in case he weary the audience with excessive celebration (*N*. 5.51). He must observe the dictates of relevance, and escape the breezes that will drive the song from the course it should be following (*P*. 11.39-40). The dangers the sea holds represent the many pitfalls the poet must avoid. A mistaken course will involve him in too long a journey, taxing the patience of his listeners, while rocks may bring the poem to an abrupt, undesired halt (*P.* 10.51-2). The metaphor of the poem-as-vessel expresses Pindar's overall relation to his art; he is both passenger and helmsman, both the spokesman of the forces that direct his journey and the individual who dictates his particular path across the seas. He is the creator and guider of his poetic vessel, the source of its original impetus. However, the ship of poetry will continue on its journey even after the death of its navigator, ceaselessly moving on to new lands and times.

The maritime metaphor not only functions as a vehicle for Pindar's themes but also fills a vital role within the structure of the ode. The image of travel by sea serves, above all, to give precise direction to the order of material, and appears at vital points throughout its course. Many metaphors occur at the opening or conclusion of the ode, or at moments of halt and re-departure within it. Pindar gives impetus to his poem at its beginning when, in *N.* 5, he opens with the contrast between the sculptor, whose creations must always remain fixed upon their pedestals, and the poet who sends his song across the seas. Pindar, embarking on the tale of the victor's city of Corinth, sets out on a voyage of his own (*O.* 13.49). Likewise, the symbol of the anchor signifies the conclusion of a particular portion or the ode's final close when the ship of song reaches its destination (*O.* 6.101). The image of travel by sea appears at moments of transition between one portion and the next, creating a close coincidence between structure and symbol. The poet turns the ship towards a new course as the emphasis shifts from one aspect of the victory to another, and the image of Gadeira at *N.* 4.69 signals that the poet is about to conclude the mythical portion and return to the victory more immediately at hand. Pindar's reflections on the changing winds and waves that represent the uncertainty of the human lot provide another incidence of the matching of imagery to structure. While they contain the gnomic material necessary for the ode's conventional form, they also point to the re-arrangement that is about to occur within the focus of the poem itself, and changes in the skies and seas indicate the poet's own change of course. Pindar may allow his metaphors of travel to emerge naturally from within the context of the ode; in *P.* 10, the myth of Perseus' voyage to the lands of the Hyperboreans is suggested by a reference to the necessary limits all mortal travels must mark (30). The myth itself leads into the traditional maritime metaphor through which Pindar passes onto the next portion of his song (51f.). Again, at *N.* 3.26, Heracles' far-flung journeys across the sea prompt the self-address which Pindar employs at points of junction in his odes:

$$\vartheta v\mu\acute{e}, \ \tau\acute{\iota}\nu\alpha \ \pi\varrho\grave{o}\varsigma \ \dot{\alpha}\lambda\lambda o\delta\alpha\pi\acute{\alpha}\nu$$
$$\ddot{\alpha}\varkappa'\varrho\alpha\nu \ \dot{\epsilon}\mu\grave{o}\nu \ \pi\lambda\acute{o}o\nu \ \pi\alpha\varrho\alpha\mu\epsilon\acute{\iota}\beta\underset{\sim}{\epsilon}\alpha\iota;$$

My spirit, towards what foreign headland are you turning my journey?

Elsewhere, Pindar will deliberately highlight his device, inviting the audience to appreciate his skill and mastery. Just at that moment when the genre proves most difficult to handle, the point of transition from one motif to the next, he will evoke the dangers of maritime travel, and the demands it makes on the *technê* of the navigator or helmsman. His achievement in giving an impression of continuity and progression appears the greater in the light of the poet's demanding element.

The metaphor of the winds and waves which guide a man's lifetime voyage provides a good illustration of Pindar's capacity to work his imagery into every facet of his poetry's contents, structure and themes. Part encomiastic, part gnomic, part structural in aim, the symbol is a comprehensive one which touches on the creator, the subject and the poetic medium itself. For Pindar, the essence of poetry is motion, inspiring the activity that is latent in all things. The poem becomes the changing wind or wave, constantly altering its shape and form, marking stops and starts, periods of climax and periods of calm. Pindar introduces a new aspect to his representation of his medium, making it capable not only of internal growth and development, but of external mobility and adaptation. The image of the ship of poetry represents the supreme freedom the poet can claim for his art, the vessel cut loose from the moorings of space and time, capable of describing its own passage through the winds and waves in which the poetic imagination perceives symbols of its own unfettered creativity.[9]

[9] The clouds and the waves continue as a frequent symbol for the free play of the poetic imagination in modern poetry, particularly in the French symbolists, Baudelaire and Mallarmé.

7

Pindar's Paths

Pindar's odes describe travel by land as well as by sea, along the numerous paths that cross the earth. The path serves as another metaphor in the set of motifs which focus on mobility and change, and which attribute motion to the subjects of the ode and to poetry itself. Whether literal or figurative, the path permits progress, passage and meeting, the possibility of association between the individuals who dwell at either end, separated by geography and chronology. It is a flexible symbol; active, like the winds and waves, its guides the course and character of those who choose their individual way; concrete, it is the channel for external objects, conveying the people and the vehicles who travel it. Pindar distinguishes numerous levels of meaning within his metaphor, fitting each one to the subject he presents, whether the victor, the poet or the song. The path may be the road of achievement, the track of words, the broader journey of life which all men accomplish. In his use of the path, Pindar characteristically takes over a symbol familiar from Homer, Hesiod and the early lyric poets and moulds it to the particular form and function of the victory ode.[1] It serves both his encomiastic and his aesthetic ends, permitting him to express particular praise of the victor and more general themes through a metaphor which gives to the poem the sense of mobility and progression it demands.

Like the symbol of the sea, that of the path emerges naturally from within the context and contents of the ode, and Pindar introduces it in a literal capacity throughout the poem's course. Roads are of particular significance to the victor and the poet who sings his praises. Repeated journeys characterise the lives of athletes who travel from their native cities to compete at the

---

[1] For a comprehensive treatment of the symbol of the path in Greek poetry and philosophy see O. Becker, 'Das Bild des Weges', *Hermes Einzelschriften* 4 (Berlin, 1937).

Games. In competition they follow the particular *dromos* or track which the race-course describes. Pindar portrays his athletes returning to their home after the Games are done; while the victor journeys along the highway, celebrating his achievement, the defeated athlete is consigned to the smaller roads where he can hide his shame (*P.* 8.86-7). The triumphal procession itself proceeds along the road, a lengthy one which may take in the entire distance from the site of the competition to the athlete's home.

The poet's life is also one of travels; as master of the celebration rites and leader of the dance, he must sometimes have accompanied his ode to its destination. The arrival motif may be a conventional device within the structure of the ode, signalling the moment when the poet takes up the task of praise, but its generic character should not disguise the realities of the poet's itinerant existence.[2] He might travel with the victor from the venue of the Games to his native land, composing along the way. His repeated appeals to his patron's *xenia* or hospitality suggest his genuine concern as to the nature of the reception he will meet. He frequently asserts his presence as an invited guest to a city that is not his own. The actual conditions of the poet's trade generate the metaphors related to the path and Pindar represents himself as messenger (*N.* 6.57b), herald (*N.* 4.74) and steward (*O.* 13.97). He did serve as literal escort when he accompanied the victor homewards, as herald when he proclaimed his laudandus to the assembled audience. If the poet remained behind, the song travelled the necessary paths to its place of destination and at *N.* 3.76f. Pindar dispatches the ode with apologies for its late arrival. Travel, with all the unknown risks it involves, is the necessary condition for the athletic competition and for the bard, and athletes and poets are distinguished from lesser men by their willingness to take the path that leads away from home.

From the literal path, Pindar moves to the metaphoric level where roads describe the entire course of a man's existence. Every path has a beginning and an end, an *archê* and a *telos*, which symbolise the birth and death of the individual. The poet frequently refers to the journey of life which men must inevitably accomplish, making the path of human existence common to the

[2] Mullen, op.cit., p.28.

rich man and the poor, to the poet himself (*N.* 7.19-20; *I.* 7.40-2).
It is a road which must finally lead to death, down the *aguian
thnaskontôn*, path of dead men to which Pindar alludes at
O. 9.34-5. Each deed stands as a portion of the path, with its own
start and conclusion, its departure and halt. Different men
follow different courses, just as the winds and waves create
varied destinies.

Certain paths stand pre-eminent. The athlete and the patron's
path is the road of achievement, one which leads to victory or the
success that the *telos* represents.[3] Pindar portrays this journey's
end in concrete form, whether the mark which the javelin strikes,
or the Pillars of Heracles that stand at the final extremity of
every mortal act. The road of accomplishment is more lengthy
than that which most men travel, leading the individual to the
limits of his capacities (*O.* 9.105). The rewards it offers match its
greater difficulties, and Pindar introduces the notion of the
necessity of trial and effort which all success demands. He
includes athletes, poets and all men of wisdom and virtue when
he writes of the steep heights of skill (*O.* 9.107-8), evoking the
toil that precedes the most glorious reward.

The poet's path involves many of the same features as the
athlete's. However, before merging the two journeys which poets
and athletes perform, Pindar constructs another meaning to his
metaphor of the path. The poet is the man who lays down the
road along which he travels, creating an actual path of words.[4]
The epic term for song itself signifies path, *oimê*, and at
Od. 8.73, the bard relates how the Muse inspired him 'to sing the
fame of men, a song (*oimê*) whose fame now reached the wide
heaven'. Words of passage describe the bard's activity as he
composes his verse; the author of the Homeric Hymn speaks of
'moving over' to another song, while the term *dielthein* expresses
the speaker's progress from start to finish.[5] Xenophanes and
Parmenides make conscious use of the figure of the path when
they refer to embarking on a new road, symbolising their

---

[3] Becker, op.cit., p.54f.
[4] On the early sources for the notion of a path of words see K. Meuli, 'Scythica',
Hermes 70 (1935), p.172.
[5] Pindar's use of traditional poetic diction in his path metaphors is discussed in
M. Lefkowitz, '*Tô kai egô*: the first person in Pindar', *HSCP* 67 (1965), p.197 and
n.44.

intention to pass on to a different theme.[6] Pindar's *hodon logôn*, path of words (*O.* 1.110) and *epeôn oimon*, road of verse (*O.* 9.47) are no more than developments of this traditional motif which neatly complements the image of the poet who travels together with his ode along the very path of speech that it creates. He acknowledges his debt to former poets whose road of song he follows or extends, and suggests how his own track of words will guide subsequent composers. Poetry itself, fittingly, is a vehicle which travels the course of the words, as the poet accomplishes his journey in the Muses' chariot (*O.* 9.81; *I.* 2.2).

The roads of the poet and the victor coincide in the close complex that exists between word and deed, the path of song and that of accomplishment. The metaphor is an appropriate one to portray the tight bond between laudator and laudandus, expressing the reciprocity of their relationship in the shape of an object which does promote association and meeting, and which brings together the individuals who lie at its different ends. Pindar establishes parallels between the victor and the poet's path through coincidence of vocabulary; the poet can imitate the athlete's progress along the track as he describes how *anedramon humnôi*, I ran up in song (*O.* 8.54). He rises up from the ground, covering the distance of the path in the air as he executes a long or broad jump (*N.* 5.19-20). More critically, the path of song could not exist but for the path of deeds which heroes and victors establish. The poet's task is to repeat his athlete's course, and to follow in his track. Road imagery describes the interaction between word and deed at *N.* 6.45f.:

πλατεῖαι πάντοθεν λογίοισιν ἐντὶ πρόσοδοι
νᾶσον εὐκλέα τάνδε κοσμεῖν· ἐπεί σφιν Αἰακίδαι
ἔπορον ἔξοχον αἶσαν ἀρε-
τὰς ἀποδεικνύμενοι μεγάλας,
πέταται δ' ἐπί τε χθόνα καὶ διὰ θαλάσσας τηλόθεν
ὄνυμ' αὐτῶν·

There are broad avenues from every side for chroniclers to deck this island with renown; for the sons of Aeacus furnish for them an outstanding portion, displaying their great

---

[6] Xenophanes 7.1, Parmendies 2.1-2. For a discussion of the road in Parmenides see Becker, op.cit., p.139f.

deeds of merit, and their name flies from far off over the
land and sea.

The wealth of feats which the race of the Aeacidae have
accomplished makes the poet's task an easy one, while an act
unsuited to representation in song would stop him in his tracks.
In matching the deeds to roads of song, Pindar fulfils the duty
placed on him, that of giving the momentary victory or success a
lasting form. His poem permanently describes and repeats the
path of the victor's achievement, and evidence of the enduring
nature of the road of words lies in the myth and legend which
Pindar's own poetry draws on.

In reiterating the paths established by ancient bards, Pindar
suggests the power of the road of song to create a passage
between the past and present. He plays upon the motif of the
road-of-old, making it simultaneously the ancient poet's path of
words, the legendary hero's path of deeds and the line of descent
which joins the present-day victor to his mythical predecessors.
The path of achievement the hero established may assume a
concrete form; the figures of antiquity whom Pindar evokes
appear as path-finders and path-constructors; their deeds of
valour involve forging passages where none existed before,
clearing tracts of land of hostile elements and making them safe
for men to travel. Heracles was renowned for his voyages by land
and sea (*N*. 3.20f.) while Aristoteles lays out a straight and level
path which will be followed by men of future generations
(*P*. 5.90-3). Pindar describes the festivities which recall the dead
man's foundation, a lasting testimonial to his achievement. The
present-day victor travels in his ancestor's path both when he
re-enacts the deeds of prowess which brought the family its
renown and when he gives proof of the lineage to which he
belongs. The path is an obvious symbol for the notion of descent,
the direct line which joins men of the present to those of the past.
Heritage is an essential element in Pindar's presentation of his
subject, and his praise is directed not only towards the
individual athlete or patron, but to his family and predecessors.
At *N*. 2.6-7 he speaks of the ancestral road which Timodemus
follows, while Alcimides is sure of victory when he matches the
track of his grandfather (*N*. 6.15-16). The path which the present
day athlete treads continues an ancient and heralds a future one
which he or his offspring may extend. The future path serves as a

metaphor for both an athletic victory and a song yet to come when, at the close of *O*. 1., Pindar imagines the journey he will make along the road of words in celebration of a new victory won by Hieron (109-11). Paths travel in all directions, upwards and downwards as well as from past to future. The downward path takes the song to the shadowy underworld of Hades, into the realms of the dead. On several occasions Pindar evokes the image of the dead of the athlete's family who rejoice in his present success; at *P*. 5.96f., the holy kings in Hades actually hear the words of the song and delight in the new triumph:

> ἄτερθε δὲ πρὸ δωμάτων ἕτεροι λαχόντες Ἀΐδαν
> βασιλέες ἱεροί
> ἐντί· μεγαλᾶν δ' ἀρετᾶν
> δρόσῳ μαλθακᾷ
> ῥανθεισᾶν κώμων {θ'} ὑπὸ χεύμασιν,
> ἀκούοντί ποι χθονίᾳ φρενί,
> σφὸν ὄλβον υἱῷ τε κοινὰν χάριν
> ἔνδικόν τ' Ἀρκεσίλᾳ·

Apart, before the house, other sacred kings have Hades as their lot. They hear somewhere in their buried hearts of the great merit (of Arcesilaus), sprinkled with the soft dew under streams of songs, that is their wealth and a joy well-deserved and shared with their son Arcesilaus.

At the close of *O*. 14 it is not the song itself, but Echo who travels to the 'dark-walled home of Persephone' where she announces the athlete's triumph to his father. The song also reaches upwards towards the sky where it invokes the attention and patronage of the Olympians, often summoned to attend its performance.[7] While the 'bronze heavens' are forbidden to mortal men (*P*. 10.27), song can travel this upward path, tracing in reverse the journey made by the god-sent ray which granted the victor his moment of glory in the Games (*P*. 8.96). The path of song, in its travels from life to death and back to life again, between the realms of the immortal gods and mortal men suggests poetry's ability to grant its subject undying existence.

[7] Cf. Mullen, op.cit., p.86f.

Its course is not merely a linear but a circular one, and its possibility for endless repetition, departure and return makes it both a beginning and an ending.

Only certain paths merit representation in song. The road also has an ethical significance, symbolising certain moral values and giving concrete shape to virtue and vice, truth and falsehood, right thinking and wrong. It was Hesiod who first stamped on both the rugged and the smooth path a distinctively moral character, attributing goodness to the one, and evil to the other:[8]

> ... badness is to be caught in abundance and easily; the road to it is smooth and it dwells very near. But between us and merit the immortal gods have placed the sweat of toil; the path to it is long and steep, and rough at first. But when a man has reached the top, then it becomes easy, although it was hard before (*Works and Days*, 287-92).

The steep road in Pindar is also indicative of the virtue of the man who chooses it, of his willingness to expend toil and effort in pursuit of his goal. While the way remains difficult, a sense of the value of the task may smooth the course (*I.* 2.33-4). A man can recognise the path of virtue through the brightness of its appearance (*O.* 6.73). It also takes clarity of mind to distinguish the right path, and men who have lost their wits frequently mistake their way. The road becomes a symbol of the path of thought that is internal to man and which guides him towards accurate or confused perception. When the cloud of forgetfulness overcomes the men of Rhodes at *O.* 7.45 it *parelkei pragmatôn orthan hodon/ exô phrenôn*, draws aside the straight path of deeds from their wits, and they risk falling into the error and ignorance of the blind. The poet's role in indicating the correct path for men to follow is a critical one; by virtue of the powers of memory which he enjoys, the gift of the nine daughters of Mnemosyne, he perceives the paths of past, present and future events. He dispels the darkness of forgetfulness or misrepresent-ation, and teaches men which are the correct roads to travel. The poet's responsibility is a grave one since the path of words itself may lead a man towards good or ill; at *N.* 7.23-5 Pindar evokes the moral significance of his task when he relates how tales may

---

[8] Becker, op.cit., p.59f. for further examples of the use of the rough and the smooth.

'lead astray' or correct the blind illusions which most men suffer from.

The capacity of words to influence men for good or evil depends on their character and shape. The truthful word describes a straight path, the deceitful one a crooked. The tradition of words that assume the configuration of the ideas they represent is an archaic one, and the upright and the bent are the two major categories which describe the moral nature of speech. The Homeric judge is the one who speaks *ithuntata*, in most straightforward fashion (*Il.* 18.508), and in Hesiod words that lie are termed *skolioi*, crooked (*Works and Days* 194). Pindar creates the image of the man of straightforward speech (*P.* 2.86), a foil to the devious sycophants who also exist within the city's government. The notion of uprightness lends itself to a double metaphor; it is a quality which, according to Plato's later formulation, indicates both standing up straight and being correct.[9] Pindar frequently conflates the two ideas, evoking the straight path which represents goodness and truth, and the upright moral stance or walk of the man who travels it. The poet is the individual who may unite both facets, travelling straight along the direct course of words. The expressions *diorthoô*, to make straight, and *orthos*, upright, apply in Pindar to descriptions of the poet's task (*O.* 3.3; *O.* 7.21; *I.* 3/4.55-7). He sets his song upright in providing the correct account of the deeds that he narrates. He may remedy a crooked version given by another. The character of the path he travels depends, in part, on his own moral stance. His manner of walking serves as a means of characterising his mental disposition, and the poet may adopt the circuitous path of the wolf when he addresses his rivals and detractors. His progress with regard to his patron must, however, always be an upright one (*P.* 2.83-5). Walking metaphors allow him to indicate his piety as he refuses to progress any further when the path of a particular tale would lead him into speaking evil of the gods (*O.* 1.52). He likewise 'stands aside' when he reaches a point of human wickedness, too awful to be related in the ode (*N.* 5.16). The positioning of the limbs and body is of particular relevance to the context of the song; the poet celebrates the athlete, the man who combines both rectitude of mind and body and who, in his training, is

[9] *Laws.* 7.803d.

concerned with achieving the correct alignment of his arms and legs. In running, jumping, wrestling and throwing the javelin, the body's stance is critical to his success. The dancers who may have performed the ode must imitate the victor's positioning, maintaining straight spines, legs and shoulders. Both dance and athletics are more than physical exercise, and demand qualities of mind as well as body. Dancing will play an important role in Plato's vision of the ideal training for the citizens of his Republic, and he uses the parallels between the upright mind and straight body when he speaks of the dances of peace and war which will take place:

> In these dances the quality that is upright (*orthon*) and well-extended – given that it is in imitation of good bodies and souls, and that the limbs of the body are for the most part in good alignment – is the quality that is considered correct (*orthon*) and its opposite incorrect.
>
> (*Laws* 7.815a-b)

The poet is the individual responsible for the co-ordination of all these elements, of the motion of the dancers, the upright character of his tale, the moral pointers towards good conduct it must contain. The song assumes the ethical character of the man it represents and the man who creates it, clear with the light of truth, steep in the heights of skill it describes, direct in accordance with the shape of its ideas.

In evoking his path of song, Pindar also indicates the structure of the verse. The notion of travel belongs at once to the arrangement of the material and the passage between the elements the poem contains. Pindar signals the movement from the athletic present to the heroic past through the metaphor of a journey, from the *archê* of the starting point of the hero or family's fortunes, to the *telos* at which the divine favour becomes manifest, the theme for the song both among poets past and contemporary. Pindar may use the pattern of strophe, anti-strophe and epode to make his stages clear; he evokes the image of the path at the start of a strophe to announce that he will depart from the very beginning of a tale (*O.* 6.22) or may match the individual's journey's end with an arrest in the epode. Like the image of the sea voyage, the path of song permits Pindar to change direction, to pass from one portion of the ode to the next, to stop and start anew. The most obvious use of this device is at *P*. 11.38 where Pindar portrays his indecision between two possible roads as a means of moving from the myth to the victory. Twice Pindar uses verbs which signal halts in order to drop one theme and pass onto the next, disguising his poetic ruse under the cover of piety (*N*. 5.16; *O*. 1.52). The metaphor of the Muses' chariot also serves to guide the progress of the ode as Pindar mounts his poetic vehicle in embarking on a fresh portion of his journey (*O*. 9.80f.).

The metaphor of the path does not simply provide an image of the journey of the poem itself. Perhaps in addition to describing the structure of the material, the road imagery had a role in the element of dance the epinician ode involved. The dancers too perform a journey, that which is dictated to them by the poet in his role as choreographer. Although we know nothing of the actual movements the *kômos* performed, the many verbs of motion which appear throughout the ode may also have served as instructions to the chorus, directing their beginnings and endings, pauses and resumptions as their steps and motions coincided with the changing stanzas.[10] Neither they nor the song describes a purely linear path, and the circling motions they perform imitate the ode's own circular chronology and ring composition. The *kômos* provides a visual realisation of the poem's mobility, and of its capacity for return as well as departure, a guarantee of its enduring nature.

The path is another symbol which Pindar introduces at every level of his ode, including in its scope the laudator, laudandus and the audience at large in addition to the varied elements of song and dance. In tracing movements in every direction, the song indicates its own facility for travel across the divisions of gods and men, life and death, words and deeds. In understanding the Pindaric ode as a journey along the road, as the poet invites his audience to do, we may see how he maintains an impression at once of logical progress and impromptu composition. While the path inevitably travels from start to finish, whether its course is a straight or circular one, there is ample place for the novel and unexpected along its route, for short-cuts and diversions. Like so many of Pindar's symbols, the path may also be seen in relation to the nature of metaphor itself, and to the representation of victory it creates; the road is a possible means of imagining the

---

[10] On ancient accounts of the triadic dance see Mullen's Appendix, pp.225-30.

behaviour of poetic discourse, with its repeated passage between different levels of meaning, between the literal and figurative material and themes. In metaphor, the word traces a path from its place of normal usage to a novel one, developing along the course of its travel. The path as a whole may likewise be regarded as the linguistic continuum, on which the individual word or thought imposes an artificial distinction. The experience of victory which Pindar portrays is likewise all of a piece, and the poet sets himself the task of discovering the relationships between its varied elements.

8

Landscape

Pindar's odes never lose sight of the victor and his achievement which must remain the true centre of the epinician song. This victory does not stand in isolation but is part of a wider complex which involves events of the past and future, places both present and remote. The victor and his triumph bear a particularly close association with two groups of men, heroes and the poets who celebrate great deeds in song; the former provide a paradigm for the athlete's own acts of prowess, a model which he follows and repeats. The latter give lasting form to these acts, and establish them as a visible pattern in their own right which men of future generations may imitate and recall. One set of metaphorical motifs focuses less on the nature of the song itself, its diverse powers and motions, than on the victor's relation to his mythical ancestors and to his laudator. This draws into its scope the diverse elements which the heroic and poetic environments include, collapsing distinctions between time and place, creature and kind. Victory, Pindar suggests, requires the broadest of all possible frames for full expression, and through metaphor may be set in meaningful contrast and comparison with the features which make heroes and the poet who sings them pre-eminent among men.

The landscapes of poetry, heroics and athletics are distinctive ones, invested with many religious, mythical and ethical levels of meaning. Landscape is a flexible concept in the climate of Pindar's day, and one which, like the natural elements, lends itself readily to metaphoric representation. Indeed, metaphor alone can accommodate the many unknown and unfamiliar regions that poets might evoke. The very topography of Greece prohibited men from gaining an accurate perception of the environment, leaving great tracts of uncharted land to the imagination of the myth-maker and bard. Mountains and woods separated the centres of population, and frequently the sea was the easiest means of travelling from one part of the land to another. No term in the Greek vocabulary can take in landscape in its entirety, neither *topos*, place, nor *chôros*, ground;[1] it appears as a composite of its parts, not as a synoptic whole. Like the forces of nature that shape it, landscape is familiarised and explained through anthropomorphic metaphors which people it with living presences and account for its most curious or frightening features. Seen largely as a threatening, obstructing presence, landscape has no intrinsic value and rarely appears in early poetry as a discrete element in itself.[2] Here it is either idealised or made the vehicle for the emotions and concerns of the poet and his subjects. Because it lacks a concrete identity, landscape proves a versatile tool that the poet can use at will, giving it significance or emphasis in accordance with his poetic themes. It is only when man has become sufficiently familiar with his environment that he can regard it as something outside himself, and that it may assume its status as a worthy independent poetic subject.

Pindar's treatment of landscape belongs within this overall approach. He creates an environment quite his own, and one which corresponds to no known place. His is a generalised sketch, often relying on one brief detail to describe the setting of a scene, or a traditional epithet to situate his subject. Landscape remains of secondary importance at most moments, subordinate to the themes the poet wishes to evoke, to the deeds and fortunes of the athletes, heroes and poets who form the real matter of the odes. Pindar's settings lack internal coherence, and are subject to rapid modifications in accordance with the character and fortunes of those who populate them. They assume features which serve only as symbols of human aspirations, limitations and achievements. Even the actual cities where the patrons and poet dwell and the very real sites where the Games are held are invested with religious and mythical overtones which transform their appearance and make them vehicles for abstract themes. The recognisable rivers, fountains and mountains which exist in

---

[1] W. Elliger, *Die Darstellung der Landschaft in der griechischen Dichtung* (Berlin, New York, 1975), p.1.

[2] Few treatments of landscape in early Greek poetry exist. Among the most useful are Elliger, op.cit. with comprehensive bibliography, Adam Parry, 'Landscape in Greek poetry', *YCS* 15 (1957) pp.3-29, and the collection of relevant material in K.D. White, *Country Life in Classical Times* (London, 1977).

town and countryside become artificial creations, the particular possession of the poet and the forces which help him in his artistry. Pindar, finally, has no interest in the *locus amoenus*, the place that is lovely in itself, and celebrated in terms of its own beauty. Where natural pleasance does appear in his song, it too is charged with symbolism, myth and morals. The usefulness of this fluid, changeable landscape lies in its ready accommodation of the many planes on which the poem moves and its willingness to accept a diverse population of men, gods and beasts, and the numerous creatures who inhabit the realms in between.

Pindar's landscape divides into a number of distinct environments, some benign and welcoming, others hostile and threatening. Each bears some relation to the laudandus, and serves as a fitting backdrop to his achievements. The city is impressed with the character of the victor, and the events connected with the celebration of his triumph. It is the place from which he departs to perform his feats of excellence, and to which he returns when his trial is done. A man's city is an integral part of his heritage, and must be named and praised within the 'naming complex' of the ode. It often serves as an independent motif in itself, when Pindar dwells on its history, its foundation and merits. The city carries several levels of significance to the victory at hand; its features often prove an extension of the glory the athlete has achieved, and form a strong contrast to the threatening forces which lie beyond its walls, forces which the victor has to overcome in reaching his end. The city's appearance is characteristically a bright and sunny one; fair weather and light are traditional symbols of safety and harmony in Greek thought, the attributes which the individual enjoys by virtue of his trials.[3] The city proves a haven against the darkness and the storm that lie without. The city is also important as the dwelling of the patron, deriving its status from the magnificence of its buildings. Pindar celebrates his rulers in terms of the palaces, roads and temples that their towns possess, and gives particular attention to the house of his laudandus. At the opening of *N*. 9, he declares: 'We will go in procession,

---

[3] On the symbolism of light see R. Bultmann, 'Zur Geschichte der Lichtsymbolik im Altertum', *Philologus* 97 (1948), pp.1-36; D. Tarrant, 'Greek metaphors of light', *CQ* n.s. 10 (1960), pp.181-7; and M. Treu, 'Licht und Leuchtendes in der archaischen griechischen Poesie', *Studium Generale* 18 (1965), pp.83-97.

Muses, from Apollo at Sicyon, to the newly founded city of Aetna, to the rich house of Chromius where the doors flung open are overcome by the crowd of guests.' Courts and banqueting halls appear at *N*. 1.19-24 and *O*. 1.17 where they are the scene for the rejoicing which the victory generates. Pindar also raises the theme of *xenia*, the guest friendship on which he depends, and in evoking opulence and hospitality intimates the nature of the welcome he hopes to receive at his patron's home.

The present-day appearance of the town stands as a testimonial to the acts of foundation and building which the real and mythical ancestors of the laudandus performed. Details of the cityscape are made a vehicle for a further theme, the continuity that reaches back from the present day victor to his heroic precedents who first established the city in which he lives. In *P*. 5.90-3, Aristoteles lays down a road, straight, paved and well-frequented. Psaumis constructs homes for his people in *O*. 5, leading them out of confusion and into the light that belongs to civilised existence within the city walls (14). The heroes and builders of the past continue to live on within the town, and its sacred sites express the power of the victory to reawaken and recreate the achievements of the past, spanning the realms of the living and the dead. The hero shrine is often an important element which Pindar selects from the available features of the city in giving emphasis to the continuing presence of the dead amid the present celebrations. The Aeginetan odes possess a particular wealth of such detail, expressing the close continuity between the present-day victor and the race of heroes who preceded him. They contain several references to the hero shrine of Aeacus which, according to Pausanias, lay at the centre of the agora of the island's principal city (2.29.6). *N*. 5 concludes with the command to bring crowns to the front door of Aeacus (53-4), crowns destined for the athlete's grandfather and perhaps a reference to the statue of the dead hero which may have stood before the shrine as was customary with dedications of athletic sculpture.[4] *N*. 8.13-16 again speaks of the chorus as suppliant at the knees of Aeacus, and again the act of crowning unites the living athlete with the dead. Thus Pindar brings into play the mythical and religious overtones of his city site, presaging the

[4] Mullen, op.cit., p.76.

lasting nature of the celebration which the present-day victor will enjoy.

Buildings and shrines also feature at the site of the athlete's victory, the venue of the Games. The name of the competition must be included within the contents of the ode, and Pindar may focus on the sacral nature of the place in order to reinforce the glory of the men who compete there. The sites of the Games draw both gods and heroes into their scope, the divinities who oversee the events and heroes who first founded and administered them to honour the gods. In *O.* 10, the landscape of Olympia is made the subject of the central myth itself, and each feature of the sacred setting is viewed in terms of the pattern of divine events which brought about the site's establishment. It is no mere place for athletic competition, but a sanctuary and sacred precinct. Such descriptions highlight the religious aspect of the Games, their character as cyclically recurring festivals which glorify the gods as well as the athletes who achieve their victory there. Like the city, the place of the Games is secure from incursions from the wilder elements of nature. In *O.* 3, Heracles brings into existence a series of consecrated places through which the poem moves in its description of the site. The language emphasises the wilderness that prevailed before the hero's acts of clearing and foundation, and the gentle loveliness of nature that exists there now.[5] The sacred precinct which the Games' site represents echoes the other dwelling place of the gods, the meadows and fertile gardens which Pindar's poetic patronesses haunt.[6]

Through his symbolic representation of the landscape, Pindar establishes links between events involving heroes of the past and athletes of the present, between victors and gods, patrons and poets. He draws into one complex the many places which the ode's leaps from reality to myth and past to present must accommodate, discovering connections between them which are largely the product of his poetic imagination. Landscape thus seemingly reinforces the coherence of the poem, making the victor's place in a broader mythical and religious context appear a natural one. In *O.* 1, Pindar draws on the fact that Olympia

---

[5] On the landscape symbolism in this particular ode see C.P. Segal, 'God and man in Pindar's *First* and *Third Olympian odes*', *HSCP* 68 (1964), p.228f.

[6] Cf. T.G. Rosenmeyer, *The Green Cabinet: Theocritus and the European pastoral lyric* (Berkeley and Los Angeles, 1969), p.188 and n.32.

was a colony of 'Lydian Pelops' (24), and that Pelops was the hero buried at the site of Hieron's triumph. Pelops is the subject of one of the myths that Pindar includes in the song. *Olympian* 6 draws together a host of even more disparate sites, discovering links between them through myth and metaphor. Pindar must mention the Sicilian colonial residence of the patron, in or near Syracuse, but also alludes to the Peloponnesian mother city, Stymphalus in Arcadia. The song itself travels between the two, from Stymphalus to Syracuse (98-100) and from the poet's native Boeotia to Sparta where the victor's family had its remotest origins. A mythological connection is established between Thebes and Arcadia, binding victory, poet and myth into a close complex which all but defies logical representation. The links which *P.* 5 establishes between Cyrene and the victory at Delphi are more straightforward; Pindar draws on curious elements of Delphic topography, its cypress chamber (38-42), to create a parallel with the origins of the cult of Apollo Carneius at Cyrene which the ode relates. It was the hero Battus, mythical founder of the city, who adorned the place and established the cult (89-93). The mythical and religious events that take place at a particular site serve as both its defining characteristics and as the elements through which Pindar creates continuity in landscape.

Beyond the city and the sacred site of the Games lie the uncharted regions of the forest, mountain and sea. The descriptions of these areas stand in stark contrast to the harmonious and safe city dwellings, and serve as metaphors for the other faces of victory, the strife and turmoil it involves.[7] While within the city walls man is master of his environment and of himself, without he is the plaything of external forces which lie beyond his control. Pindar thus creates a dark foil, evoking landscapes particularly symbolic of threat and disorder. Darkness characterises the forest and wooded mountains, the black-leaved trees which Mount Aetna bears (*P.* 1.27). It creates a sense of isolation and disorientation, and dark landscapes are instantly evocative of Hades, the sunless realm of the dead where confusion prevails. The topos of nocturnal solitude is a conventional one and Pindar's heroes often face their moment of

---

[7] For a cross-cultural treatment of threatening landscapes see Yi-Fu Tuan, *Landscapes of Fear* (Oxford, 1960).

greatest personal difficulty against a night-time setting.[8] Pelops
dares to brave the solitary night in order to achieve the highest
rewards available to men:

> ἐγγὺς [δ'] ἐλθὼν πολιᾶς ἁλὸς οἶος ἐν ὄρφνᾳ
> ἄπυεν βαρύκτυπον
> Εὐτρίαιναν·
>
> (*O.* 1.71-3)

Drawing close to the white-flecked sea alone in the
darkness, he called on the loud-pounding god of the
splendid trident.

A similar scene occurs in *O.* 6 where Iamos goes by night to
invoke the god Poseidon to his aid (61). Shadowy landscapes hide
the true path from men, and Pindar cautions against passing
into the mists that lie beyond Gadeira (*N.* 4.69). Voyages are
notoriously dangerous because of the hostility of the sea, an
element which symbolises danger and misfortune as men chart
their way through rocks and whirlpools, buffeted by winds and
waves. The sea may even threaten the city, and attempt to
overthrow its precarious harmony. At *O.* 6.100-1 Pindar
combines the maritime with the nocturnal landscape when he
cautions:

> ἀγαθαὶ δὲ πέλοντ' ἐν χειμερίᾳ
> νυκτὶ θοᾶς ἐκ ναὸς ἀπεσκίμ-
> φθαι δύ' ἄγκυραι.

It is good that in a stormy night two anchors be thrown
down from the swift ship.

A mountainous setting likewise is a hazardous one, where men
may encounter threatening creatures and infringe on realms
reserved for the gods alone. The construction of the opposing
poles of town and countryside, of harmony and turbulence,
permits Pindar to represent the individual's passage from toil to
glory as a journey from one environment to the next. In *P.* 9, both
the Nymph Cyrene and the victor Telescrates undergo trials in

---

[8] On this topos see Segal, op.cit.

the rugged setting of northern Greece before coming southwards to a land portrayed in all its fertility.

The appearance of the landscape is determined by the epoch as well as the state of the man's fortunes who passes through it. A particular environment signals a shift from the present day to a mythical age, and the wilderness beyond functions as a symbol of archaic times when men still lived in close proximity with natural forces and had constantly to overcome their hostile setting. Indeed, the wilderness provides the hero with the opportunity to perform his mighty deeds, and serves as an integral part of his subsequent renown. An early association with rugged landscapes characterises many of Pindar's heroes and presages their later status. The relationship between the child and his natural setting may be a benign or antagonistic one, but the mere fact of his birth or upbringing outside the city walls sets him apart from ordinary men. Euadne leaves her palace home in order to give birth to Iamos in the boundless brake where he lies amid the cluster of violets (*O*. 6. 53f.). He continues his association with untamed nature until the moment when he invokes the god and assumes his rightful heritage (*O*. 6.58f.). Cheiron's many mythical protégés grow up in mountainous surroundings and, in the lands around the Centaur's cave, encounter wild beasts. Jason leaves his childhood home for the city dressed in the leopard skin which recalls his exploits in the mountainous environment (*P*. 4.81), and Cyrene likewise frequents the *oreôn keuthmônas skioentôn*, the hollows of the shady mountains, before her departure as Apollo's bride (*P*. 9.34). Pindar takes the material the mythical tradition has devised, and uses it to establish the contrast between the harmony that victory may provide and the dangers that necessarily precede the tranquillity that the victor or hero earns. The athlete too must suffer the trials which take concrete form in the hero's struggles with his environment, and likewise pass outside the city realm to run the extremes of risk and danger.[9]

Pindar also draws on the wider ethical significance a man may see in his landscape. The universe was understood as an ordered hierarchy, under the dictates of the gods but prone to occasional dislocation and reorganisation. Radical changes in the landscape

---

[9] K. Crotty, *Song and Action* (Baltimore and London, 1982) for the athlete and hero's departure from the city into the untamed realms of nature, p.113f.

are a result of evil and rebellion which assume a physical reality.
Threatening phenomena, eruptions, eclipses and the like, are
made symbols of the misdeeds among men and gods, and natural
disasters the manifestations of the divine wrath such deeds
provoke. The fate of Typhon, trapped beneath Mount Aetna as a
punishment from Zeus, demonstrates the consequences of
pitting oneself against superior forces.[10] The monster's wickedness expresses itself in the activity of the volcano:

$$ποταμοὶ δ' ἁμέραισιν$$
$$μὲν προχέοντι ῥόον καπ'νοῦ$$
$$αἴθων' · ἀλλ' ἐν ὄρφναισιν πέτρας$$
$$φοίνισσα κυλινδομένα φλὸξ ἐς βαθεῖ-$$
$$αν φέρει πόντου πλάκα σὺν πατάγῳ.$$

(*P*. 1.22-4)

In the daytime rivers pour out a blazing stream of smoke,
but in the darkness of night a crimson flame rolling down
carries rocks to the wide expanse of the deep sea with a
crash.

Pindar repeatedly warns men against seeking to compete with
the gods, and finds in the landscape actual features which serve
as symbols for man's aspirations and the limits he must observe.
Certain regions are prohibited to men, and even the mighty
Bellerophon is refused passage beyond the boundary the sky
represents. The bronze heavens, the dome of Olympus, do not
admit mortals except with divine consent, as in the case of
Heracles. The seas as well as skies set their own borders to mortal
endeavours; at one extreme lies the land of the Hyperboreans, a
place where even Perseus was only permitted a brief stay. In the
far west stand the Pillars of Heracles, actual rock formations
which the myth of the hero's travels provided an account for.
Far-flung travels symbolise courage and nobility of character,
the generosity a man displays (*I*. 2.39-42). However, genuine
wisdom lies in recognising the bounds which the natural world
casts up.

[10] The opening portion of *P*. 1 is built about the antithesis between the
harmony the lyre promotes and the divine order which Apollo and the Muses
represent, and the anarchy and chaos that prevail among those 'that Zeus loves
not'.

A truly harmonious landscape is one in which there is a perfect concordance between a man and his environment. Here he has no need to struggle against it, or to transform it in order to achieve an idyllic existence. Pindar draws on a tradition which makes of natural growth and luxuriance a reflection of equitable relations between men and gods; in both the mythical Golden Age and such miraculous lands as the Islands of the Blessed the earth is naturally fertile and gives up its produce without interference on the part of man.[11] The advent of agriculture, according to one view, did not mark progress, but rather came as a punishment on men who were forced to damage the earth in search of food. The deeds of colonisation and foundation which the heroes performed were only necessary when men had exhausted or been refused the resources formerly available to them, and the very exercise of human power over nature was a reminder of man's antagonistic relationship with his natural setting. The poet looks back to this idyllic landscape in his portrayal of the victor in his triumph and the poet on his own quest for, and creation of, song. The setting in which he and his fellow bards move contains many echoes of the Golden Age, when not only poets but all men lived in close harmony with the gods. Pindar finds within his individual landscape all sources of poetic nourishment; the springs and fountains which he frequently alludes to are holy places, incarnating the multiple powers of the poet and his art, its capacity to refresh the men it celebrates, its mirror-like reflection of great deeds, its power to promote the growth of fame, and his naming of Dirce often serves as an assertion of his poetic vocation. The Theban poet honours the Muses' spring throughout his verse, drawing from it the inspiration which permits him to compose his songs:

πίσω σφε Δίρκας ἁγ'νὸν ὕ-
δωρ, τὸ βαθύζωνοι κόραι
χρυσοπέπ'λου Μναμοσύνας ἀνέτει-
λαν παρ' εὐτειχέσιν Κάδ'μου πύλαις.

(*I.* 6.74-5)

---

[11] Rosenmeyer refers to the 'Golden Age nostalgia' among the ancients, 'an aristocratic scheme contrived when new political and social developments threatened to destroy the influence of noble lords and caused them to look back with longing to a remembered glory'. Rosenmeyer, op.cit., p.215.

I shall give him to drink the sacred water of Dirce which the deep-girdled daughters of gold-robed Memory have made to spring up beside the well-fortified gates of Cadmus.

Other forms of liquid nourishment appear within the poet's landscape, fostering men and plants alike. Dew is a natural promoter of growth and refreshment, and honey was envisaged as a kind of dew which fell from the skies on the leaves of the plants and trees below. This was an important substance for men of the Golden and the heroic age, as well as an indispensable source of the poet's mellifluous voice. The natural gardens and meadows Pindar occasionally evokes possess a sacral character in Greek thought, ready haunts for the poet who makes of their flowers and fruits symbols for his creativity.[12]

The poet draws on every possible aspect of the landscape, building on traditional associations and discovering new significance. He evokes the wilderness of mythical and archaic times, and the city symbolic of victory over the threatening forces without. The poet's possession of his own garden or grove reaches from Hesiod through Pindar to modern poetry, suggesting a broader aesthetic aim. The poet's 'green space' serves as a retreat from a world of ordinary reference into one of flexible meaning where every object is invested with multiple associations, each feature of the landscape capable of suggesting new patterns of relations. Through the landscape metaphor, the poet leads our imagination back to a time when there was unity between man and his environment, bringing about the recreation of the Golden Age which Blake saw as the aim towards which all poetry must tend.[13] Pindar's landscape sets the world of divinities and heroes within the present context, interweaving epochs and conditions inside the own particular setting that his imagination creates. Pindar's poetic landscape finds an echo in the grove which Keats will subsequently build, in which the later

[12] The notion of a distinctive landscape for poetic creation is discussed in B. Snell, op.cit., ch.16. See also C.P. Segal, 'Horace *Odes* 2.6: poetic landscape and poetic imagination', *Philologus* 113 (1969), pp.235-53.

[13] Discussed by N. Frye in *The Educated Imagination* (Toronto, 1963), p.21. Metaphor, which for seventeenth-century writers was a sign of paradise lost, is described by Frye as the instrument of 'return', the 'language of identification through which poetry tries to lead our imagination back to the identity figured in the stories of the lost Golden Age, Eden or Hesperides'.

poet likewise performs his acts of creativity. Addressing Psyche rather than the Muses he writes:

> Yes, I will be thy priest and build a fane
>   In some untrodden region of my mind,
> Where branchèd thoughts, new grown with pleasant pain
>   Instead of pines shall murmur in the wind
>
> And in the midst of this wide quietness,
>   A rosy sanctuary will I dress
> With the wreath'd trellis of a working brain,
>   With buds and bells and stars without a name,
> With all the gardener Fancy e'er could feign,
>   Who breeding flowers, will never breed the same.

(Ode to Psyche)

9

Birds and Beasts

The landscape in which poets, heroes and athletes move also holds a place for birds and beasts. Within the poetic settings Pindar creates they appear both as actual creatures and, more frequently, as metaphors for the distinctive qualities and attributes of the men whom Pindar portrays. They serve to characterise the particular experience of the athlete, with whom they are compared and contrasted, and to establish parallels between him and the heroes who often possess close associations with the animal world. Animal and bird metaphors are also brought to bear on poetic composition, offering symbols of the powers which Pindar claims for his own art, and acting as a natural source of the song which the poet creates. Thus they function as a link between the spheres of poetry and victory in the Games. The many tenors the animal carries points to its particular suitability for metaphoric representation; it provides both a reflection and a distortion of human character; at once like and unlike man, the animal kingdom offers the closest vantage point from which men can view their own behaviour, drawing analogies and contrasts.

Poetic, mythical and moral traditions had long used the beast as symbol, and Pindar draws freely on earlier representations. Animals appear in the genre of the fable which takes the creatures of the earth and air and uses them as a means of passing comment on human types and conduct. The Greeks ascribed the beast fable to Aesop, a legendary figure thought to have lived some time in the sixth century B.C.; although the collection of his tales was not compiled until the Roman Empire, many stories have their origin in Babylonian, Aramaic and Egyptian texts and iconography far older than Aesop himself.[1]

[1] The question of the sources of Aesopic fables is treated in M. West, 'Near Eastern material in Hellenistic and Roman literature', *HSCP* 73 (1969), p.113-14. Also see H. Lloyd-Jones, *Females of the Species*, op.cit., pp.21-2.

The fable appears in very early Greek poetry, in Hesiod, Archilochus and Semonides, and some of the animals whom Pindar portrays belong to fabular traditions. Animals had long played an important role in myth as well as fable, often closely involved in the lives of the gods and heroes whom Pindar himself evokes. His use of the animal as metaphor also finds a clear precedent in the Homeric simile where it serves as a vehicle for the poet's broader themes and concerns. Here animals are neither merely the humorous representations of types of human behaviour, nor the fabulous creatures of myth, but a model and reflection of the hero's thought and deeds. In the simile they act in mainly symbolic capacity; while retaining their distinctive animal identity, they seem to become the expression of more abstract forces, an image of the play of human temperaments and emotions.[2]

Pindar uses the metaphor of animals and birds as a means of distinguishing between men and of portraying the different levels of behaviour and feeling which may co-exist within the single individual. Two features of the Greek view of animals make them particularly suitable vehicles for Pindar's themes; one concerns the ambiguous attitude the Greeks held towards the animal realm, now admiring, now fearful, the other the generic quality they attributed to animal character. The behaviour of the bird or beast made it symbolic of the wild, untamed side of nature which threatened men, a world dominated by *phusis*, natural instinct, in which *nomos*, man-made law, had no sway.[3] To act like a beast, in the Greek understanding, was to stand outside the norms that civilised life prescribed and to return to the conditions that existed before man gained his fully human status, characterised by the use of speech, fire and technology. This same state of nature was, under another perspective, an idyllic time when men lived in close harmony with their environment, a part of the Golden Age which Pindar seeks to recapture in his landscape of metaphors.[4]

---

[2] On the animal simile in Homer see Coffey, op.cit., Fränkel, op.cit. and A. Schnapp-Gourbeillon, *Lions, héros, masques, les représentations de l'animal chez Homère* (Paris, 1980).

[3] M. Detienne, 'Between beasts and gods', in Gordon, op.cit., pp.218-19.

[4] Cf. P. Vidal-Naquet, 'Plato's myth of the statesman: the ambiguities of the Golden Age and of history', *JHS* 98 (1978), pp.132-41, where the author shows how the paradise of the Golden Age was imagined as an animal paradise.

Animals remained a part of the unity which men had since divorced themselves from, and the refusal to eat meat, the flesh of animals, later distinguished such sects as the Pythagoreans who sought to regain this primal harmony.[5] The animal may thus serve as an expression of both savagery and nobility, two important notions in Pindar's treatment of individuals who stand somewhat outside the daily norm, the athlete, victor and poet. It can take the form of foil or analogy, representing the worth of the man whom Pindar celebrates or the wickedness of those who stand against him. The symbol of the animal is also useful in providing a fixed representation of whatever characteristic Pindar wishes to focus on.[6] According to the Greek view, each species always displays the behaviour thought indigenous to its kind,[7] and Pindar emphasises the unchanging character of his animal symbols:

> τὸ γὰρ ἐμφυὲς οὔτ᾽ αἴθων ἀλώπηξ
> οὔτ᾽ ἐρίβ᾽ρομοι λέοντες διαλλάξαιντο ἦθος.

(O. 11.19-20)

But neither the tawny fox nor loud-roaring lions ever change their inborn nature.

Immutable in nature, animals represent a fixed hierarchy of values against which Pindar measures his characters and describes the different relations between them. The animal acts as a shorthand for certain kinds of human behaviour, the lion as the embodiment of courage and of might (I. 3/4.63), the ape of comic mimicry and the grotesque (P. 2.72).[8] The fox and wolf frequently belong to the world of politics and intrigue where they symbolise treachery and cunning. The wolf-walk which Pindar adopts in P. 2.84-5 may be a traditional way of designating the gait of an enemy. Although a man may assume the guise of a variety of creatures, Pindar maintains the view that he cannot

---

[5] On the refusal to eat meat as a symbolic act of return to a previous age see P. Vidal-Naquet, 'Land and sacrifice in the *Odyssey*', and M. Detienne, 'Between beasts and gods', in Gordon, op.cit., pp.82 and 218f.

[6] For accounts of the characters attributed to different species see D'Arcy Thompson, *A Glossary of Greek Birds* 2nd ed. (Oxford, 1936), and O. Keller, *Die Antike Tierwelt*, 2 vols (Leipzig, 1909-13).

[7] B. Snell, op.cit., p.186f. The same point is taken up by Lloyd, op.cit., p.184.

[8] W.C. McDermott, 'The ape in Greek literature', *TAPA* 66 (1935), pp.165-76.

change his basic nature. The animal symbol provides a ready way of expressing this fundamental theme, carrying the notion of the unshakeable distinction between *ho sophos* and *hoi mathontes*, the man possessed of innate merit and those who merely learn their skills. The individual born without genuine talent or worth can no more acquire it than the animal can change its nature, and crows stand as opposites to eagles (*O.* 2.86-8), and lions to foxes (*O.* 11.19-20). The clash of characters and types is cast in the form of contrasting animals who, unlike men, do not even pretend to adopt a behaviour other than that they are born with.

Different species of animals span the full range of possible human characters, from the basest to the most noble. In many cases, men who act as beasts represent the opposition that heroes, poets and athletes must face in performing their deeds of merit. Animal vocabulary used of men often carries a pejorative note, suggesting that the individual has gone beyond the norms men should observe and has joined a lower order. Archilochus feeds animal-like on slander (*P.* 2.55-6), like the lesser poets who would seek to rival Pindar's might. Pindar himself asks that he escape the *dakos adinon*, sharp tooth, (*P.* 2.53), the bite or sting of a savage beast. The negative exempla which Pindar evokes as warnings for his laudandus likewise display beast-likē conduct; Ixion becomes little better than an animal in his pursuit of Hera which reveals the basest of his instincts and he himself becomes the prey of Zeus, caught in a trap like an animal (*P.* 2.39f). Hunter and hunted imagery appear throughout this ode, remarkable for the quantity of animal symbolism it contains.[9]

Greek myth devised symbols for the co-existence of antithetical impulses within a single figure in the shape of creatures who combined elements of both animal and humankind. The Centaur, half man, half horse, carries within one body contrasting and conflicting natures, and its rapid descent into unruly, anarchic behaviour portrays the shifts all human conduct can display.[10] Cheiron, a central figure in several

[9] Cf. M. Lefkowitz's treatment of *P.* 2 in *The Victory Ode* (New Jersey, 1976), pp.8-42.

[10] Pindar's reference to the centaurs is discussed in P. von der Mühll, 'Weitere pindarische Notizen', *MH* 25 (1968), pp.226-9. For a broader treatment of the centaurs in Indo-European traditions see G.S. Kirk, *Myth: Its Meaning and Functions in Ancient and Other Cultures* (Berkeley and Los Angeles, 1970), pp.152-62.

of the myths Pindar narrates, stands apart from the rest of his race; he represents a supremely civilised life, master of every art, a nature dweller who associates with gods and with heroes. The twin impulses which the race of Centaurs expresses, both in the division between Cheiron and the rest, and in their shape itself, are alive in all men but most obviously apparent in the heroes of myth and legend whom Pindar uses as the models for his athletes. Animals frequently play a distinctive role in their lives, present already in their infancy where they presage future prowess, and act as a suggestion of the forces the hero will one day harness and display. The relationship between the beast and the infant may be a nurturing one; Iamos is fed by two snakes on the 'harmless venom' of the bee at *O*. 6.46-7, and the chthonic snake combined with the symbol of honey serves as a portent of the prophetic gifts the child will later acquire. Heracles' encounter with the snakes sent by Hera appears on several occasions in Pindaric myth and allows the infant its first display of heroic might (e.g. *N*. 1.39f.). Achilles, Jason and Cyrene all grow up beneath Cheiron's tutelage and, in the mountainous landscape where he dwells, they hunt down wild beasts, lions, deers and panther. Pindar ignores the tradition that would have Achilles devour the raw flesh of the animals he slays,[11] but does portray him in the chase:

$$\{ \dot{\varepsilon}v \} \ \mu\acute{\alpha}\chi\alpha \ \lambda\varepsilon\acute{o}v\tau\varepsilon\sigma\sigma\iota v \ \dot{\alpha}\gamma^{\iota}\varrho\sigma\tau\acute{\varepsilon}\varrho\sigma\iota\varsigma \ \dot{\varepsilon}\pi\varrho\alpha\sigma\sigma\varepsilon v \ \varphi\acute{o}v\sigma v,$$
$$\varkappa\acute{\alpha}\pi^{\iota}\varrho\sigma\upsilon\varsigma \ \tau^{\iota} \ \dot{\varepsilon}v\alpha\iota\varrho\varepsilon\cdot \ \sigma\acute{\omega}\mu\alpha\tau\alpha \ \delta\dot{\varepsilon} \ \pi\alpha\varrho\grave{\alpha} \ K^{\iota}\varrho\sigma v\acute{\iota}\delta\alpha v$$
$$K\acute{\varepsilon}v\tau\alpha\upsilon\varrho\sigma v \ \dot{\alpha}\sigma\vartheta\mu\alpha\acute{\iota}v\sigma v\tau\alpha \ \varkappa\acute{o}\mu\iota\zeta\varepsilon v$$

(*N*. 3.46-8)

In battle with savage lions he dealt death, and slew wild boars. Then he brought their bodies panting for breath to the Cronian Centaur.

The hunting, tracking and slaying of wild beasts furnishes a paradigm for the athlete, as he too contends in trials of strength, seeking the metaphoric prey that victory represents. While the Homeric simile imagines the encounters between heroes as the combat of two animals, both intent on the destruction of the other, strife and competition in Pindar are confined to the

---

[11] Cf. D.S. Robertson, 'The food of Achilles', *CR* 54 (1940), pp.179-80.

stylised struggle in the ring. The same qualities distinguish athlete, hero and animal, swiftness of foot and strength in arm and limb. The rigours of the athletic competition call on forces within the athlete which stand on a par with those the hero displays in his labours.

Like the Homeric hero, Pindar's athlete stands above the everyday world of men, and his merit requires a broader backdrop than human comparison alone can provide. Pindar looks to a realm beyond that of men, and uses the animal kingdom as both sufficiently close to and distant from the man he praises, aggrandising further through likeness and contrast. In seeking images for the individual he must celebrate, Pindar evokes the animal in all its majesty, making the species he selects an example of *aretê*, excellence, in his field just as the victor is in his. He chooses superlatives wherever they may be found: the eagle is the swiftest of birds, and fleetness of foot an essential attribute of the man who wins his victory in the race. The creature's range of flight makes it pre-eminent, matching the length of the victor's jump or cast with the javelin, and both athlete and bird accomplish journeys to the furthest reach of their ability (*N.* 5.21). The eagle also symbolises perpetual motion, the ceaseless activity characteristic of the victor in pursuit of his goal or the race's end. Even when apparently at rest, slumbering on the sceptre of Zeus, the bird's body still quivers and its wings are swift (*P.* 1.6f.). Pindar seeks his images of excellence in the sea as well as the sky, and the dolphin, the most rapid of swimming creatures, serves as another representative of the athlete's speed. Pindar remarks of the trainer Melesias at *N.* 6.64:

> δελφῖνι καὶ τάχος δι' ἅλμας
> ἴσον ⟨κ'⟩ εἴποιμι

To the dolphin through the ocean spray I would compare him in speed.

Eagle and dolphin elevate the victor far beyond mere human prowess, and only the divine outstrips them in their course (*P.* 2.50-1). Pindar's selection of his symbols is, moreover, firmly rooted in the athlete's world: a mechanical bronze eagle and a dolphin were mounted on the starting gate of the stadium at

Olympia, respectively flying up and down when the mechanism of the gate operated.[12]

Throughout Pindar's poetry, the same metaphorical motifs apply to victor and poet both, signalling the relationship of mutual dependency that exists between them. The flexible nature of the symbols he selects permits Pindar to express two subjects in one metaphor, passing over distinctions in creature and in kind. The animal may represent excellence simultaneously in several spheres, and through use of one metaphor Pindar lays claim to the same virtue and abilities as the man he celebrates. When poet and athlete both assume the guise of birds, both become creatures possessing extraordinary strength, speed, agility and range, the literal attributes of the athlete, the figurative ones of his laudator. Like the athlete at the starting point, or the bird ready for flight, Pindar stands 'poised on light feet' (*N.* 8.19). He selects flight rather than song as the cardinal attribute of the bird, describing himself not as the shrill-voiced nightingale in the tradition of other poets,[13] but as an eagle surpassing all other birds in its range as does the athlete in the competition. With a motion as swift as the bird he emulates, Pindar passes from the athlete to the poet as the tenor of his metaphor, and presents eagle and athlete in quick succession as joint images for the singer's art:

εἰ δ' ὄλβον ἢ χειρῶν βίαν ἢ σιδαρίταν ἐπαινῆ-
σαι πόλεμον δεδόκηται, μακ'ρά μοι
αὐτόθεν ἅλμαθ' ὑποσκά-
πτοι τις· ἔχω γονάτων ὁρμὰν ἐλαφ'ράν·
καὶ πέραν πόντοιο πάλλοντ' αἰετοί.

(*N.* 5.19-21)

If it seems best to praise wealth or strength of hands or iron war, let someone dig for me here a long leaping pit: I have a light spring in my knees and eagles fly beyond the sea.

The parallels that Pindar's metaphors establish permit him to speak in the same expression of laudator and laudandus and the closing image of *N.* 3 describes the one seizing his theme as a

---

[12] M.I. Finley and H.W. Pleket, *The Olympic Games* (London, 1976), p.28f.
[13] E.g. Hesiod *Works and Days* 208; Bacchylides 3.98.

bird to its prey, the other snatching victory from his opponents
(80-1).[14] Pindar's birds need not represent exclusively either the
athlete or the poet, and to assign a single term of reference to an
image is to mistake the fluid character of the Pindaric metaphor
which conflates and compresses, building unities where none
previously existed.[15] The eagle is symbolic of merit wherever it is
found, the lesser crows and jackdaws vain imitators of its
unattainable prowess.

Pindar attaches the animal kingdom to the poet's realm, to
song as well as to the epinician poet. Animals stand in close
association with music and with verse. The poet, like the animal,
is part of the natural landscape, and acts of composition
frequently take place within a pastoral setting where birds and
beasts provide an audience for the harmony produced. Tradition
makes the poet a shepherd, and the Muses initiate Hesiod into
his task while he is tending his lambs beneath Helicon
(*Theogony* 22-3). Pan and Orpheus play to the creatures of the
land and air, and the Greeks attributed to animals the power to
recognise the true musician and Aelian describes the unmusical
ass and the bee who would fly in the direction of pleasing sounds
and shrink from the discordant note.[16] The dolphin appears in
Pindar's accounts of athletic prowess, the bee in his
representation of song (*P.* 10.53-4) and the mule when he is
forced to work this most prosaic creature into the contents of
O. 6, and so yokes it to the poetic chariot (22). The response of
the animal to music reflects the broader role that melody fulfils,
maintaining a deeper, cosmic harmony which penetrates all
things, human, animal and divine.

The animal does not only serve as an audience for the
musician's creations, but as a model for his activity; the natural
outpourings of the bird act as an image for the ease of

[14] M. Lefkowitz, 'Bacchylides' *Ode 5*: imitation and originality', *HSCP* 73
(1969), p.56, n.14.

[15] Controversy exists concerning the identity of the eagle and the crows in
Pindar's metaphors. R. Stoneman, 'The Theban eagle', *CQ* n.s. 26 (1976),
pp.188-97, argues that the birds represent not Pindar and rival poets but the
victor and his opponents. For a convincing refutation see P.A. Bernardini,
'L'"aquila tebana" vola ancora', *QUCC* 26 (1977), pp.121-6.

[16] Aelian, *On animals*, 10.28, 5.13.

composition the poet should achieve, and the nightingale in full song appears as a metaphor for the poet in Hesiod and Bacchylides. Bees and poets both are termed *liguphthongos*, clear-voiced, perhaps because the ceaseless humming of the insect was thought harmonious.[17] The voice of the bird or bee is of less concern to Pindar than the motion which the creature represents; birds and beasts are masters of the environment in which they move, and inhabit the winds and waters from which the poet draws his inspiration. Their use of the natural forces gives to the creatures a mobility which poetry seeks for itself.

Birds rise up on the wind, symbols for the ease of passage which will enable the Pindaric song to spread the fame of the victor to every corner of the earth. Pindar claims for his poetic skill the wings which permit the bird to master its element (*N*. 7.22). In the case of the bee, Pindar likewise focuses on its motion as it passes among the flowers, and the poet describes how his songs of praise 'flit' like the insect from blossom to blossom (*P*. 10.53-4). Winged creatures of every kind have particular relevance to song by virtue of the ancient identification between words and flight;[18] in Homer speech which comes from a character's *thumos* flies from him to his listener while words which are unspoken remain 'wingless' within. Song becomes a winged force capable of promoting flight in others and may carry a man airborne onto other victories; at *I*. 1.64, Pindar asks that his laudandus may triumph again,

> εὐφώνων πτερύγεσσιν ἀερθέντ' ἀγ'λααῖς
> Πιερίδων

rising up on the shining wings of the fair-voiced Muses.

Wings and feathers also create a place for the bird alongside other common Pindaric metaphors for song, more firmly rooted within the athletic context of the poetry. Pindar frequently represents his ode as a wreath, and feathers resemble the leaves which make up the crown of triumph and the foliage which men

---

[17] On the bee and its role in poetry see J.H. Waszink, 'Biene und Honig als Symbol des Dichters und Dichtung in der griechischen-römischen Antike', *Rheinisch-Westfälische Akademie der Wissenschaften* Vortrage G., (Opladen, 1974).

[18] *Od*. 15.445, 17.57. On 'winged words' see Onians, op.cit., p.67f.

cast at the victor. At *P.* 9.123-5, Pindar uses the terms for feathers and for leaves interchangeably in his description of the practice of pelting the athlete with leaves, which celebrates a success. A similar association of ideas lies behind the metaphor of *O.* 12.15 where Pindar conflates the feathers of the bird with the foliage of the victory wreath. The single verb *kataphulloroeô* describes the cock shedding its plumage and the plant losing its leaves, both images of decline which the eternal wreath of song negates.[19] The same feathers suggest another Pindaric metaphor, that of the winged arrow of song which the poet shoots from the bow he claims from Apollo and the Muses. The shafts which he delivers serve as further indications of the power of poetry to cross vast distances, for divine and poetic arrows transcend normal divisions of time and space. Like a bird to its prey, the arrow finds its mark, the victor whom it is Pindar's role to celebrate in everlasting song.

Pindar's metaphors never lose sight of the poet's duty of praise, and the symbol of the animal or bird as song gives further expression to this theme. In *N.* 3 the eagle metaphor serves as a statement of *kairos*, of Pindar's ability to select from the wide range of material exactly that which is relevant and appropriate to the occasion at hand. The quality of *kairos* involves the length and brevity of the song, the correct proportions of praise and caution, the observance of propriety. The animal becomes the symbol of Pindar's ability to find the right path of song which will satisfy all these demands as he bids the charioteer yoke up the mules of Hagesius' winning team to the figurative vehicle of song at *O.* 6.22-5.

Song, Pindar suggests, has a close affinity with the gods who were the original practitioners and possessors of the art and continue to involve themselves closely in the poet's task. The animals who serve as metaphors for song and for the creative process reinforce the links between the poet and the immortals since they too are often the favoured creatures or representatives of the god who watches over the singer's craft. Birds, by virtue of their powers of flight, come closer to the Olympians than any mortal, and often serve as symbols of the gods in myth and iconography. At one time the gods may even have been thought to assume a bird-like shape for their travels to earth, and

[19] Cf. Nisetich, op.cit., p.262f.

Homer's immortals often appear as winged creatures when they travel down from Olympus.[20] Pindar describes the semi-divine Boreads who came to the aid of Jason and the Argonauts as:

> ἄνδρας πτεροῖσιν
> νῶτα πεφ'ρίκοντας ἄμφω πορφυρέοις.

(P. 4.182-3)

men, with purple feathers rippling about their backs.

The bird is the channel of communication between gods and men, the earth and sky, and brings portents and signals from the divine which the augur interprets (I. 6.49f.). Individual species are associated with particular gods, and the eagle serves as the symbol for Zeus on whose sceptre he slumbers in P. 1.6. The bird's winged passage between the earth and heavens makes it a fitting emblem for the possibility of travel to realms still inaccessible to men. Like the song which may journey on into the future, and create an undying existence for those it celebrates, the soul, on leaving the body after death, is sometimes imagined as a bird, winging its way to a new life in unknown lands.[21] The bee is also associated with the forces of death and regeneration, and embodies the souls of the dead who 'hum in swarms' when they leave the mortal body.[22] Bees also enjoy the particular patronage of the Muses and of Apollo when they appear in connection with another related gift, that of prophecy. Pindar terms the Pythia the *Melissa Delphidos*, the Delphic Bee (P. 4.60), communicant of the divine will to men. Another animal who spans both Olympian and chthonic realms is the horse, favoured creature of Poseidon, the lord of the arts of charioteering and navigation which feature so prominently in Pindar's account of his poetic composition.[23] The horse is a

---

[20] Coffey, op.cit., p.120, n.29.

[21] Representations of the soul as a bird about to take flight are common to many Indo-European traditions. According to the *Anthologia Palatina* 7.62, the tomb of Plato was marked by an eagle symbolising his soul flown to Olympus.

[22] Sophocles, fr. 799. A.B. Cook mentions gold bees found in Crete and Etruria intended to be represent the immortal soul. See 'The bee in Greek mythology', *JHS* 15 (1895), p.19.

[23] On horses and their role in cult see F. Schachermeyr, *Poseidon und die Entstehung des griechischen Götterglaubens* (Bern, 1950).

common figure in myth, achieving a semi-divine status in the case of Homer's Xanthus or the winged Pegasus on whom Bellerophon makes his ill-fated attempt to scale the Olympian heights (*I.* 7.44-7). Horses in Pindar are the particular gift of the divine and respond only to handling by poets, gods and athletes. The dolphin is another of Poseidon's creatures, responsible, one myth relates, for finding Aphrodite for its master. The essential feature that Pindar describes is the place these animals hold among the gods, and their ability to pass between the worlds of the mortal and the divine, the living and the dead. Their affinity with the gods is a natural result of their separate status from men; gods and animals frequent the same realms and share in powers denied to those who occupy the middle rank in the gods, men, beast hierarchy. Both live in easy harmony with the forces that animate their natural surroundings and are untroubled by the frontiers that limit mortal travels. The poet, hero and victor, by virtue of their particular merit, have contact with the animal world as well as the divine and lay claim to some of the faculties that gods and beasts possess. While animals may be vehicles for the savage and bestial side of human character, more often they represent the higher instincts and abilities men can display.

The animal metaphor, like the landscape, focuses principally on the victor's achievement, always the centre of the ode, and brings to mind the many areas which his triumph touches. Because of the close relationship between the laudator and laudandus, the symbolic representation of the one extends to the other. The metaphor serves as a good illustration of Pindar's faculty for building bridges between different realms through his imagery, taking from the animal its association with poetry and with heroic legend, and bringing the two together in the figure of the athlete celebrated in song.

10

The Athletic Metaphor

In making metaphors of athletics, Pindar draws on what is most immediately at hand, the event which is the occasion for the ode's composition and performance. The aim of the epinician is to give lasting form to the deed of a moment, and the poet achieves his end by bringing the weight of mythological exempla and the self-proclaimed power of his song to bear on the individual experience. In adding these further elements, Pindar transforms the particular event into an idealised, generalised representation of all instances of participation, toil, struggle and triumph and carries into its sphere all those whose performance, historical, mythical or poetic, will contribute further glory to the athlete's own. Metaphor permits the poet to project the vocabulary of the Games into every area of his audience's experience, describing the whole course of the lives of men through the various features of the athletic competition.

The athletic metaphor draws on an activity which already enjoyed a broad significance in the intellectual and social climate of the age. Athletics held a critical place in the lives of individuals and the community, and was thought essential for both internal and external harmony.[1] The central role of physical exercise manifested itself in the gymnasium, a focal point in the city where free men might meet and talk and train. Along with the agora, the temple, shrines and theatre, the gymnasium was one of the city's most important sites.[2] Athletic training contributed to the city's strength; it prepared young boys and men for warfare, and in Sparta was uniquely devoted to that end. It was also of importance for more peaceful pursuits, and for the

---

[1] For general discussions of the role of athletics in Greek Life see H.A. Harris, *Greek Athletes and Athletics* (London, 1964), and relevant information in W. Jaeger, *Paideia* (Oxford, 1939).

[2] On the central position of the gymnasium see Harris, op.cit., p.149.

individual well-being of the citizens. The combination of athletics with the arts would, according to Plato, prove the ideal education, promoting excellence of body and excellence of mind. Indeed, 'the most perfectly musical and well-tempered man, as we commonly may designate him, is he who mixes gymnastics and music most nobly, and applies them to his soul with the best sense of measure' (*Republic* 3.412a).[3]

The Games themselves involved the additional element of competition, the *agôn* so central to Greek life and thought.[4] The contest appears in very early myths and epic, and numerous accounts of competition among gods and among heroes point to the importance of this means of settling rivalry and dispute. Indeed, the contest and the awarding of prizes at its close may even have served as a very early form of law, adjudication and the redistribution of goods.[5] The athletic competition provided an outlet for both aggression and sportsmanship, and was given recurrent form in the shape of the four Panhellenic Games which are the occasions of Pindar's victory songs. Like athletics itself, the Games enjoyed wide religious, social and political importance;[6] they were early expressions of the unity of the land, a meeting place between men of different city states, and religious festivals which celebrated gods and commemorated heroes common to all the Greeks. The participants in the events might themselves enter the legendary corpus, and certain early victors became the focal point of local cults, invested with wide-ranging powers of good and ill.[7] Triumph in the contest was not a feat of athletic skill alone, but carried with it all the religious and ethical significance which the Games themselves bore.

Pindar seeks to make the athlete's experience central to everyman's life, portraying the glory of the achievement by lending it all possible relevance to the world beyond the Games.

---

[3] Cf. Mullen, op.cit., p.56f.

[4] On the agonistic element in Greek life see J. Burckhardt, *Griechische Kulturgeschichte* vol.I (Berlin 1898-1902), p.319f.

[5] L. Gernet, 'Jeux et droits (remarques sur le XXIIIe chant de l'*Iliade*)', repr. in *Droit et société dans la Grèce antique* (Paris, 1955), pp.9-18.

[6] General works on the Olympic and the other Panhellenic Games include E.N. Gardiner, *Greek Athletic Sports and Festivals* (London, 1910), and Finley and Pleket, op.cit.

[7] Cf. J. Fontenrose, 'The hero as athlete', *California Studies in Classical Antiquity* vol.1 (1968), pp.73-104.

He promotes the exchange by making the event represent in microcosm the predominant features of the human condition, and views the life of the athlete as the paradigm all men of virtue should emulate. He selects the common elements of every event, struggle, competition, failure and success, and projects them into every portion of his verse. In universalising the picture, Pindar rejects specific detail and looks not to the particular, but to what is abiding in participation and victory. Pindar's verse is remarkable for the scarcity of concrete detail it contains, and the poet largely ignores the drama of the occasion he is called on to represent. Even Bacchylides gives a fuller account of the atmosphere surrounding Hieron's victory than Pindar who refers merely to the abstract qualities of the man he celebrates.[8] Pindar treats athletics as he does his other sources of metaphor, taking from the Games their moral and spiritual significance and setting aside what is too immediate or particular. One feature of the athletic experience which Pindar discerns in every human life is competition; the agonistic motif appears in the form of the struggles waged between individuals, and between man and the abstract forces which stand in his way. These contests are part of the much broader one carried on at the cosmic level where competing forces lock and wrestle, good against evil, lies against truth, slander against deserved praise. Pindar uses a metaphor drawn from the wrestling match when he describes the struggle between Hesychia and Hubris where the goddess casts her opposite into the bilge (*P.* 8.11-12). The ring where the boxing and wrestling events took place are miniaturised representations of a society where *eris*, strife, both good and bad, prevails. The race track also provides an image of the course of human life; men race in unending pursuit of their goals, some attainable, some impossible when 'our limbs are fettered with vain hopes' (*N.* 11.45-6). Struggle and pursuit necessarily involve pain, and Pindar finds in the element of toil a further link between the experience of the athlete and the general pattern of mortal endeavours. True success, in whatever realm it is achieved, comes only at the price of struggle and effort while the reward which is won without effort is no true prize (*O.* 5.15-16; *O.* 6.9-11). At *N.* 7.74, the poet passes from the athletic metaphor of the javelin thrower to a generalised statement of the

---

[8] Bacchylides 5, written to celebrate the same event as Pindar *O.* 1.

relation between pleasure and pain: *ei ponos ên, to terpnon pleon pederchetai*, if there is pain, the greater pleasure follows. Pindar moves from the actual trial of the athlete to the outcome of his attempt; all competition inevitably ends in success or failure, the brief *mochthôn ampnoan*, rest from toils, (*O.* 8.7) or breathing space such as the athlete might take between events. Good fortune and ill appear in the terminology of triumph and defeat, and the act of crowning or the victor's wreath become symbols for success in every sphere (*P.* 1.100). Prosperity is seen as an extension of the particular delight that victory brings, and is expressed through the same metaphors of agonistic victory. The terminology of defeat in the Games likewise describes every instance of reversal or hindrance. Images of tripping, stumbling, being held or thrown signal the frustration of a man's designs as he falls victim either to his own inner nature or to the superior forces, concrete and abstract, which stand in his way. Pindar sets the individual against his antagonist at *N.* 4.39-41, and describes the defeat of a goal in terms which recall the thrown man struggling in the dust.[9]

From his generalised portrayal of the agonistic elements in human life, Pindar turns to the particular case of those who stand in closest proximity to the athlete, namely the hero and poet. Through the athletic metaphor, he constructs a series of parallels between their experiences, setting them in analogical relations to one another. The Games are of relevance to the hero in a religious, quasi-historical sense. Heroes may be responsible for their actual foundation, and *O.* 3 and 10 recount Heracles' role in initiating events at Olympia. They serve as a re-enactment and commemoration of the hero's life and their origins were thought to lie in the competition held around the tomb or pyre of the dead man. The hero would be pleased by the spectacle of men engaged in acts which he himself enjoyed while still alive and in which he frequently excelled.[10] The cyclical nature of the Games ensures a constant remembrance of the dead man's deeds and through the festivities he is made to live

[9] M. Poliakoff gives a closer analysis of the wrestling image in this passage and *N.* 4.93-6; *Studies in the Terminology of Greek Combat Sports* (Meisenheim, 1982), p.137f.

[10] The question of the funeral origin of the Games receives further discussion in E.N. Gardiner, 'The alleged kingship of the Olympic victor', *BSA* 22 (1916-19), p.86.

again. The ode itself evokes the hero both in mythical allusions and in references to the actual hero shrine where he lies buried; often the language itself suggests that the ode was intended for performance in the vicinity of the shrine, and that the hero's presence was a literal reality which poet and *kômos* would acknowledge through word and gesture. Pindar's song addresses the holy kings down below as he reminds them of the common prosperity and triumph they share with the living victor who is their son (*N*. 5.96f.).

More specifically, the life of the victor involves the same pattern of toil and reward as that of the hero, and the actual trial recalls the mythical *agôn* which formed so important a part of his status. The same distinguishing features characterise both; a willingness to risk all in pursuit of the greatest of rewards which a man may achieve, an undying *kleos*, that particular fame which is celebrated everlastingly in song. The Argonauts choose a life of renown over one without danger, even at the price of possible death (*P*. 4.185f.), and Ergoteles decides not to remain in his native city (*O*. 12.13f.). Pelops rejects a peaceable old age for the struggle which will bring him far greater returns (*O*. 1.82-5). Heroes, like victors, do not achieve their ends without considerable effort and pain. Peleus undergoes numerous trials before receiving his prize, while Heracles, the mythical founder of the Olympic Games, combines the suffering and joy that are the common experience of the athlete. He is the supreme example of the man who toils unremittingly, but wins a reward commensurate with his pains. Similar demands are made of the hero and athlete in terms of skill and prowess, and Pindar establishes further parallels between the two by using terminology which belongs to the athlete's exploits in the event where he competes. The hero must be fleet of foot and mighty in his arms and limbs. He is unerring in his casts, and so swift that he has no need of dogs in the hunt (*N*. 3.50-1). In place of the athletic opponent, the hero meets his foe in the form of a wild beast, or contender on the field of battle. He is athlete, hunter, warrior all in one, and the present day athlete is no more than a particularised version of this archetypal superman.[11] Pindar places war and athletics on a par, proclaiming a man's excellence in both spheres. The race of the *doriktupôn Aiakidan*,

---

[11] Cf. Fontenrose, op.cit., p.73.

spear-clashing men of Aegina, at *N.* 7.9-10 find their just reflection in Sogenes' triumph in the pentathlon, and athletics stands midway between the extremes of war and more peaceable pursuits such as the cultivation of the Muses' arts.[12] The hero's success is not the result of his might and skill alone but, like the athlete, he is the recipient of divine favour. In the experiences of both, Pindar pinpoints the moment of god-given delight, represented as a beam of light suddenly illuminating the darkness. It may be solicited, as in the case of Pelops or Iamos, or come unasked, quite suddenly. The god may simply appear by the hero's side as witness to his act or may address him directly. Gods communicate through dreams and oracles, natural prodigies, through gifts of winged horses or an immortal bride. Often this moment of grace lies at the central point in the structure of the ode, the pivot on which the particular relationship between the hero and victor turns.[13] The acts of both men cast light on one another; the divine gift which lies in the mythical past is made visible by the recent evidence of the athlete's own victory in the Games, while the athlete's achievement grows in splendour by virtue of this additional glory. The heroic paradigm allows the laudandus and the audience to appreciate the full significance of the moment of triumph, and suggests that the deed they have been witness to will stand on a par with that of the hero. The language of the Games and of the epic past interact with one another, collapsing distinctions in time and character.

Another individual whose character and experiences make him a fit counterpart to the athlete is the poet himself. He likewise performs his task by virtue of three elements, innate talent, god-given favour and the skill that is refined through practice and effort. Pindar claims for himself a worth which contrasts with the imitative skill of his rivals (*O.* 2.86), and is possessed of a nature which gives him a predisposition for his task. He is also dependent on the particular guidance which the gods bestow, and his invocations of the Muses and other deities within the poem's course provide evidence of their indispensable role. The poet, like the athlete, would be nothing if divine aid forsook him, and he claims the patronage of the Muses who give

---

[12] Mullen, op.cit., p.61f.
[13] Ibid., pp.100-9.

him clarity of vision (Fr. 52h.15-20). The intervention of the gods may come suddenly, as in the case of the athlete or hero, when the deity invoked stands by the side of the poet and his chorus. Song is a divine-sent radiance into whose light the poet passes, emerging from the darkness of the storm (*I.* 7.37-9).

No two realms are so intimately related in Pindar as those of song and sport. The poet repeatedly portrays his essential part in the athlete's triumph, suggesting that the lasting renown of the individual depends not on his deed alone but on its celebration in song. His fame shares in the worth and renown of the poet commissioned to write the ode. Poetry and athletics are such complementary activities, Pindar suggests, that the terminology of the one suffices to describe the other, binding laudator and laudandus together in the complex of mutual need and association that *N.* 7.11f. describes. Pindar participates with his subject throughout the course of the experience, matching him both in the event and in the celebration that follows. Poetic composition involves the poet in running (*O.* 8.54), jumping (*N.* 5.19-20), charioteering (*O.* 6.22), throwing the javelin and discus (*O.* 13.93-5; *N.* 7.71). Wrestling describes the struggles he must wage against his opponents, whether fellow poets who compete with him for patronage or more abstract hostile forces. His encounters with his rivals are portrayed in agonistic terms, himself the winner, his rivals the losers (*P.* 1.45). The poet also competes with the demands of his genre (*N.* 4.93-6), seeking to satisfy the many requirements which stand as rules in the Games. A mastery of the laws of the epinician permits Pindar to strike the Muses' target, the ideal of song (*N.* 9.55), and he must keep his chariot of poetry along the correct track as the charioteer in the race. Pindar constantly draws attention to the fact that his song has not contravened the limits that must govern it, and at *N.* 7.71 asserts that he did not overstep the mark in casting his javelin, an act which would disqualify him from the event. The poet who fails to fulfil his role acts like an opponent in the Games, and praise justly or unjustly uttered is often expressed through agonistic metaphors. At the close of *N.* 7, Pindar declares:

τὸ δ' ἐμὸν οὔ ποτε φάσει κέαρ
ἀτ'ρόποισι Νεοπτόλεμον ἑλκύσαι
ἔπεσι·

(*N.* 7.102-4)

But my heart will never say that I have dragged down
Neoptolemus with ruthless words

in an image of dragging some part of the opponent's body
forward in an attempt to upset his balance, a frequent strategem
in the palaestra. The poet victorious in completing his task of
praise is represented as having overcome his opponent
(*N.* 4.93f.). Like the athlete's experience, the poet's is a
strenuous one, demanding skill and expenditure of energy. The
sportsman competes only after he has mastered his event
through rigorous training and practice, and certain still existing
papyri suggest how exacting his preparation might be, with rules
and stratagies to be learnt for every sport.[14] The skilful handling
of his material which Pindar points to through athletic
metaphors makes the activities of laudator and laudandus
complementary ones.

Once the trial is done, the poet resumes his individual identity
and participates in the events which celebrate the triumph. He
mingles with the crowd who proclaim the victory, raising his
voice in the cry of joy which greets the athlete (*N.* 7.75-7). The
poet's act of composition and song becomes an integral part of
the celebratory rites; the poem is the victory wreath with which
the poet crowns his laudandus and the praises it contains fall
about the athlete like the leaves and flowers cast at him in the
triumphal processions. At *O.* 9.108, the song is represented as
the actual prize in the Games, and elsewhere takes on various
shapes and forms which suggest the rewards the victor might
have received. Victory and song become one when the athlete is
proclaimed in his native city and Hieron crowns Ortygia with
wreathes, both the literal garlands he has won and the figurative
flowers of praise (*P.* 2.5-7). Song assumes its true importance for
the athlete when his trial is done, transforming the pain of
competition into the delight of triumph through its proper

---

[14] Poliakoff, op.cit. On the *technē* and training required of the poet, see the
reference given in Crotty, op.cit., p.142, n.49.

composition and performance. It enables the athlete to rest from his exertions and to forget the struggle they involved, becoming in turn a drink which would slake his thirst (*N.* 7.61-3), water to soothe his tired limbs (*N.* 4.3-5) and wine which brings forgetfulness of pain (*N.* 9.50f.). The poem carries subtle intimations of future victory and renewed flowering at the close of *O.* 1, encouraging the laudandus on to further prowess and merit which the poet will again celebrate in song. One further link binds poet to subject at the event's end, the gracious reception both hope to receive in the athlete's native town where the ode will be delivered. In asking the city to welcome home the victor, Pindar claims for himself the same gift of hospitality.

Within the city, the poet's song becomes performance, the words, music, and dance which the epinician involves. The role of the *kômos*, like that of the poet, stands in complementary relationship to the athlete, imitating both the retinue that would have accompanied the hero of the legendary past and the actual group who would have served as an escort to the athlete on his homeward return. The *kômos* performs what is, in some sense, a re-enactment of the trial and triumph as the poet's language describes the labours of competition, the moment of victory, and the celebration that followed immediately on the event. Although it is impossible to recreate the motions and gestures of the *kômos*, the Greek view equates dance with the feats of athletics the epinician describes. Dancing is itself a mid-point between the two activities which the genre unites, music and athletics, and is, according to Plato's later account, divisible into two elements, dancing as wrestling and dancing in itself (*Laws* 7.795e).[15] The latter joins two further aspects, uniting a decorous imitation of the Muses with physical exercise concerned with fitness, nimbleness and grace. Dance thus becomes an integral part of the meaning of the ode, a celebration at once of the hero in his deeds of might, the victor in his athletic skills and the poet, practitioner of *mousikê*. The dancers of the *kômos*, frequently young boys of the same age as the youthful athletes, provide visual representations of the contestant and his deeds, and, in the steps and movements they describe, train

---

[15] Athenaeus 1.20 relates how Socrates would tell his friends that dance had the advantage of providing exercise for all the limbs at once. Also see Aristophanes, *Frogs* 729. Mullen, op.cit., p.57.

their own bodies for excellence in battle, the Games and in the arts.

The athletic metaphor may be seen as a unifying one which draws into its scope the literal event, the mythical paradigm, the role of the poet and the choral band. Characteristically, Pindar constructs the complex through internal echoes in the language and imagery of the verse, and the athletic metaphor functions at the structural as well as the thematic level of the ode. Often a single motif recurs throughout, enabling Pindar to keep the athlete and his triumph at the centre of the song while passing through apparently disparate episodes and themes. The event in which the victory was achieved dictates the choice of vocabulary. *O.* 10 celebrates Hagesidamus, winner in the boy's boxing match. Boxing terminology ties the young boy to his heroic paradigm who is celebrated as *huperbios*, very mighty (15), *kressôn*, stronger (39) and *alkmios*, brave (44), all vital attributes in the match. Boxing also enters the gnomic and reflective portions of the ode; at the very beginning Muse and Truth are asked to use a straight blow against reproach, and later portions return to the motif of the hand, the source of the victor's triumph. The god's palm at 20-1 and the *purpalamon belos*, bolt from the firehand, at 80 assume their true significance at the poem's close where Pindar asserts:

παῖδ᾽ ἐρατὸν ⟨δ᾽⟩ Ἀρχεστράτου
αἴνησα, τὸν εἶδον κρατέοντα χερὸς ἀλκᾷ

(99-100)

I have praised the lovely son of Archestratus, whom I saw prevailing by the might of his hand.

The wrestling imagery which returns throughout *N.* 4 also emerges from the context of the event which the ode celebrates. Wrestling metaphors enter repeatedly into the poem's stanzas, establishing internal coherence between the parts. Pindar extends his motifs from the broadest application to the most local significance, from his general portrayal of human life as the struggle in the Games to the individual expression where the athletic terminology that appears is relevant only in retrospect.

The complex of poet, victor, hero which Pindar constructs within every facet of his song is an indissoluble one; the poet alone could reveal in the brief moment of victory a broader significance, seeing in its light reflections of the mighty foundational acts of the heroes of the past. By evoking these, which the present audience knows through their celebration in song, Pindar suggests how his own laudandus will enjoy the lasting fame that comes with poetry. In making the connections between the heroes and songs of the past and those of the present clear to all, the poet will bring about another victory, that of the athlete's and his celebrant's glory over time.

11

Intimations of Immortality

Throughout the various metaphors which Pindar develops, the theme of the power of song to overcome death and to grant everlasting glory to the praiser and the praised repeatedly appears. In one set of motifs, the song features as a device which establishes permanence even in the midst of transience and change. In another, poetry's powers of mobility and passage enable it to transcend the normal divisions of time and space, to rouse the dead and to travel on even into future realms. A third set places the individual in relation to the figures of the past who live on through the medium of epic, and to the poets who sing of past and present glories, and achieve their own particular form of immortality. These various elements come together when Pindar directly confronts the subject of death, negating its finality through symbols which express men's aspirations towards a future existence. He evokes the lands of everlasting life which Homer and Hesiod describe, where heroes go to dwell in perpetual joy when they have performed their labours on earth. He draws on the perfect state of immortality which belongs to the Olympians, and which they may extend to their particular favourites. Pindar also takes over the motifs involved in the actual rites and iconography of death, which symbolise hopes for a continued existence even in the act of burial and lamentation. The song becomes a talisman which turns the fate of the dead into a state of unending joy and celebration. By virtue of the word that lives and grows, the *kleos* that the poet sings becomes a lasting one which grants some form of existence to its subject even after his life is done. Through the links he constructs between victory, song and representations of death, Pindar intimates the power of his verse to create an alternative state of immortality for both laudator and laudandus.

Ancient Greek thinking about death is an amalgam of many beliefs, drawing on divergent cultures and traditions. Two major accounts of the fate of the dead exist and continue side by side in religious, artistic and literary treatments of a theme of perennial concern. According to one tradition, death involves the division of the body and soul. While the body is left behind to wither and decay, the spirit flies down to the realm of Hades where it dwells along with the other *psychai*, souls. In life, the soul has no part in ordinary consciousness, and preserves its insensate character in death where it is identified with the *eidôlon*, a ghost or phantom, the invisible but tangible semblance of the once living being. The other account of death retains the body, the centre of a man's existence while on earth, and the agent of his pleasures and pains. Greek descriptions of the delights of the Islands of the Blessed, or of the miseries of the Underworld, represent the individual in familiar shape and form, possessing both feeling and consciousness and continuing a life not so very different from that which he led on earth. While the first tradition presents the soul enduring unending lifelessness in Hades, the second includes many elements which prolong the conditions of the world above. It is a more hopeful representation which satisfies the human desire to reject death's finality, and to see it as a mere threshold which a man must cross before passing on to new realms of existence.[1]

Pindar repeatedly establishes links between victory, its celebration in song, and the different fates a man might encounter, ever aware that his patron's life and reputation will not end with his death. Intimations of immortal existence may

---

[1] For general discussions of the Greek view of death, and of the nature of man's soul, see W. Burkert, *Griechische Religion der archaischen und klassischen Epoche* (Stuttgart, 1977); Dodds, op.cit., p.135f.; M.P. Nilsson, 'Immortality of the soul in Greek religion', *Opuscula Selecta III* (Lund, 1960), pp.40-55; E. Rohde, *Psyche: Seelencult und Unsterblichkeitsglaube der Griechen*, trans. W.B. Hillis (New York, 1925/1950); and U. von Wilamowitz-Moellendorff, *Der Glaube der Hellenen* (Berlin, 1931-2). On the *psychê* in particular, Onians, op.cit., p.99f., and E. Vermeule, *Aspects of Death in Early Greek Art and Poetry* (Berkeley and Los Angeles, 1979), p.7f. There is considerable debate concerning Pindar's own views about the fate of the dead, centering about the account given in *O*. 2.56-83. It is unclear to what extent the poet is drawing on Homeric and Hesiodic notions of special privileges in the world beyond for a heroic élite, and to what extent he may be influenced by Orphic beliefs which were current in Sicily and Magna Graecia, and adhered to by the patron of *O*. 2. On Orphic beliefs see Burkert, op.cit.; G. Zuntz, *Persephone: Three Essays in Religion and Thought in Magna Graecia* (Oxford, 1971); and the recently discovered material published by M. West, 'The Orphics of Olbia', *ZPE* 45 (1982), pp.17-28.

be found within his presentation of the athlete in his triumph, and in his reflections on the character of the song which celebrates his deed. Pindar describes the moment of victory, and the role of the verse he writes, in language which belongs to traditional accounts of idyllic realms, and his metaphoric representations create a complex which leads towards the permanency of a Golden Age. The first concern of the man who seeks unending life must be with access to the lands where immortals dwell, and with his means of passage to these far-flung places. Greek tradition situates the homes of divine and legendary creatures at the far points of the earth, often in its most westerly domains. Heroes reach their islands through a variety of means, carried by gods, blown along by winds, conveyed in divine chariots. The distant travels they perform during their lifetime become the most extensive of journeys which all men experience at the moment of their death.[2] A capacity for distant voyages characterises poets and victors in Pindar, and their arrival at the Pillars of Heracles intimates the moment when they will pass beyond the borders that limit all mortal travel. While men must stop and turn about, song, which represents laudator and laudandus both, continues on its way, air-borne on the wings of the poet's skill. The poem itself takes the shape of the vehicles which lead heroes to their final homes, portrayed by Pindar as a chariot, a favouring wind or fostering wave, a bird which enjoys a limitless range of flight.

Once individuals have gained the lands that lie at the edges of the earth, they are guaranteed an existence of delight. All idyllic realms possess certain common features,[3] elements which also appear in Pindar's symbolic representations of victory and song. Triumph and poetry, his metaphors suggest, create analogous conditions for men on earth, although they may be of briefer duration. One of the most potent symbols for a state of eternal life and pleasure is unending sunlight; a solar element belongs to

[2] The notion of a journey to some remote land of the dead exists in many cultures. See F. Cumont, *Lux Perpetua* (Paris, 1949), p.278f.; Rohde, op.cit., pp.84-90; and Vermeule, op.cit., p.56f.

[3] On elements found in diverse representations of idyllic realms and Golden Ages see B. Gatz, *Weltalter, goldene Zeit und sinnverwandte Vorstellungen* (Hildesheim, 1967), and G. Nagy, *The Best of the Achaeans*, ch.9. On Greek borrowings from Egyptian accounts of the 'Ialu Fields', realms of the happy dead, see Vermeule, p.69f. and the bibliography the author provides.

many myths of the beyond in Greek and other cultures, and the permanently shining sun serves as the source of continued existence for both men and gods.[4] Olympus itself is illuminated by a bright light that is never clouded (*Od.* 6.42-6), and sunlight appears in the description Pindar gives of the land of the dead in Fr. 129.1. The unchanging light of the sun stands in contrast to the perpetual cycle of night and day which disturbs earthly existence, and dictates that human pleasure may never be longer than the passage of a day. The human condition is an ephemeral one, shaped by the shifts of light and dark, and men may never know when they will bring a sunny day to a calm close (*O.* 2.32-3).[5] Pindar paints the uncertain course of human life, and sets it against his description of the fate of the 'good' who, at *O.* 2.61f., are rewarded with the gift of days and nights of equal length.[6] Two mortal achievements do stand out against this backdrop of change; triumph in the Games appears as a ray of sun which illuminates the victor for all to see, and he himself becomes a source of the light which spreads among men. Poetry is the beacon which his fame kindles, and which in turn feeds his glory and fixes his brilliance eternally. The light which comes from the laudandus, through the poet's agency, is unquenchable.

Eternal sunshine guarantees the perfect climate which exists in the land of the gods and the blessed dead. In contrast to the winds and waves which create turbulence among mortal men, the breezes which blow in Elysium are gentle, and the land knows neither 'snows, nor heavy storms, nor rain' (*Od.* 4.566). Pindar also evokes the benign Zephyrs, the *ôkeanides aurai*, ocean breezes (*O.* 2.71-2), which come from a sea which bears no hostility towards the men who dwell on land. Only victory and song approximate these climatic conditions on earth, transforming the waves and winds into agents for progress and growth, and resolving storm into calm. Hieron in his triumph achieves that fair weather which symbolises success and inner tranquillity of

---

[4] Cf. A. Dieterich, *Nekyia* (Leipzig, 1893), p.21f.

[5] The word *ephêmeros* is used by Pindar to describe men at *P.* 8.95. For two conflicting accounts of the poet's meaning see H. Fränkel, 'Man's "ephemeros" nature according to Pindar and others', *TAPA* 77 (1946), pp.131-45, and M. Dickie, 'On the meaning of *ephêmeros*', *Illinois Classical Studies I* (1975), pp.7-14.

[6] Cf. L. Woodbury, 'Equinox at Acragas: Pindar *Ol.* 2.61-2', *TAPA* 97 (1966), pp.597-616.

soul (*O*. 1.98), and the poet and victor pass together from turbulent to fair skies (*I*. 7.37-9). Poetry alone withstands the vagaries of the climate, and remains firm in the face of the storms and rocks directed against its structure (*P*. 6.10-14). It provides the setting in which the calm the victor briefly enjoys may be eternally prolonged.

The combination of fair weather and sunlight grants the inhabitants of these idealised realms perpetual spring and summer. A flourishing plantlife characterises the lands of the fortunate dead and in the Hesiodic Golden Age the vegetation displays abundance, permanent blossom and a growth which needs no attention on the part of men. Pindar's representations describe meadows scarlet with roses (Fr. 129.3) and flowers and trees which grow in profusion for the favoured few (*O*. 2.73). The water which runs through the fertile land promotes natural life and blossom. Again victory and song possess an analogous bloom, and exist within a state of spring and summertime. The victor or hero bursts into flower at his moment of triumph, as Pindar symbolically portrays his entry into the cycle of unending brilliance which belongs to immortal life. The poet's songs likewise are flowers which grow and blossom in the gardens of the Muses, and which put out distinctive leaves and shoots. They are fostered with the waters of inspiration which nourish, in turn, the athlete's fame growing tree-like beneath the life-promoting dews. The most extraordinary feature of the plant life in the lands described is its permanence; like the inhabitants of the places where it is found, it escapes from the cycle of growth and decline which plant life on earth observes, and retains its flowers and fruits unceasingly. The inhabitants have no need to pass through winter before the return of spring, nor wait for autumn for the crops to ripen. Hesiod paints this Golden Age when agriculture was unknown, and when men were permanently supplied with nourishment:

> all good things were given to them; the gift-giving field bore them much fruit of its own accord, unstinting (*Works and Days*, 116-18).

Gold is the defining feature of the vegetation in these lands, and the combination of the plant life with the metal creates a symbol for the suspension of the normal vegetal cycle with its periods of growth and decline, fertility and fallow. Gold is the most durable of substances, the most precious among men, and the favoured material of the Olympian gods.[7] The most noble race of men whom the gods created was the Golden one, a race untroubled by old age, pain and even death. Hesiod describes how men in that time did not truly die, but were carried into something resembling an eternal sleep (*Works and Days* 116). Gold comes to function as a general metaphor for a state of immortality when life is permanently arrested at its height of bloom. The same precious substance appears in Pindar's representations of victory and poetry, forming the matter in which he builds his pillars of song (*O*. 6.1), the material with which the Muses garland their hair (*P*. 3.89). Gold also serves as the image of excellence which captures the essence of the Olympic Games themselves (*O*. 1.1).

Free from the need to work a land where crops and fruits appear spontaneously, and possessed of abundant wealth, the inhabitants of the happy realms can pass their time as they choose. Their activities mirror those of the gods on Olympus, where the presence of the Muses and the Graces promotes eternal feasting and dance (*O*. 14.9). Pindar describes the immortal race of the Hyperboreans who engage in music, dance and revelry, and the dead in Elysium who amuse themselves with board games and horsemanship (Fr. 129.6).[8] In the Islands of the Blessed, the inhabitants weave garlands and coronets from the abundant flowers and foliage (*O*. 2.74). While Pindar represents these activities in his account, the ode itself exists within an environment of celebration. Victory promotes music, song and dance, and provides the occasion for feasting and revelry which permits men to set aside their daily pursuits and participate in more pleasurable events. The image of the everlasting celebration that exists among the gods and the happy dead stands behind the momentary revelry that triumph and song allow.

If the idyllic realms that myth and poetry describe appear in Pindar as permanent representations of success, and its celebration in song, Hades, the other possible destination for

---

[7] On gold as characteristic of the possessions of the gods see E.R. Dodds, *Euripides' Bacchae with introduction and commentary* (Oxford, 1944) on lines 553-5.

[8] The tradition of the dead who amuse themselves with board games may be a borrowing from Egyptian eschatology. Vermeule, op.cit., p.77.

men after death, stands as the negation of the most striking features of victory and verse. The distinction between Hades and the realms of the gods and undying heroes repeats itself in the gulf that divides men who triumph and win renown in song from those who know defeat, and lack poetic recall. The attributes of Hades serve as a foil to Pindar's account of the powers of poetry, and the contrast between them represents a struggle between the forces of life and death. Located beneath the ground, Hades, by tradition, is a dark, shadowy place hidden from the light of the sun. Black is its keynote, like the character of Thanatos himself who covers men's eyes, robbing them of the light and sight which signify life in Greek thought. In the Underworld men exist in a state of blindness, assuming the character of Hades himself, the sightless one.[9] While brightness and vision are the cardinal aspects of song, which illuminates the way for men, dispensing light along its course, blackness and blindness describe all human failure and shortcomings in the Pindaric world. Black is the colour of defeat and blame, the gloom which prevails until the poet appears with his gift of song (*N.* 7.61). Men who mistake the path of truth, who are misled by illusion, and who accept lies for the true account, are portrayed as blind (*N.* 7.23-4). Blindness is also the consequence of forgetfulness, the dark oblivion which song alone wards off. The black waters of Lethe, which stand at the threshold of Hades in some accounts, rob men of their capacity to remember the world above, and the inability to recollect enables them to tolerate their new condition.[10] In the realms of Hades men are consigned to silence, and the shades do no more than speak in squeaks and whispers. Song, in contrast to the deathly still of the Underworld, shouts its message aloud (*N.* 7.75), breaking the silence that covers deeds of merit which want celebration in poetry (*N.* 9.6f.). Its ringing cry sets up an echo which may even penetrate the infernal depths (*O.* 14.21), defeating the powers that would rob men of their powers of recall. Silence is merited in the case of defeat or ignominy, and the failed athlete provokes no 'sweet laughter' when he returns home from the Games (*P.* 8.85-6).

In representing the antithetical powers of life and death, light

---

[9] Cf. remarks by H. Lloyd-Jones, 'A Problem in the Tebtunis *Inachus*-Fragment', *CR* n.s. 15 (1965), p.242.

[10] On forgetfulness as a water of death see Vernant, *Mythe et pensée*, op.cit., p.59f.

and dark, memory and forgetfulness, song and Hades address the continued existence of a man's family on earth as well as his individual fate after the moment of his death. Future generations represent an essential part of his glory, standing as a guarantee of the family's lasting life and continued fame. Pindar compares the fate of a wealthy man dying without an heir to that of one who goes down to Hades with his deeds unsung, and makes of both images of the absence of future life and fame (*O*. 10.86f.). Sterility prevails in the Underworld where Hades and Persephone are childless, while song continues to foster the growth of a man's name even beyond his immediate death. Poetry in its life-promoting role frequently appears in the shape of water, the cardinal symbol of fertility and regeneration. Again, song stands in direct contrast to Hades which, like death itself, is dry. In death a man was thought to lose the vital moisture, the blood which sustained him during life, and Homer characterises the living man as one who is *dieros*, wet.[11] Dead creatures sometimes seek to replace the liquids they have lost by means of the offerings they drink down, and the tradition of the thirsty dead prevails in many cultures. Other thirsty men are the Pindaric athletes and heroes who stand in need of celebration in song, parched of that additional source of moisture which continues on even after the individual has spilt his life substance on the field of battle, or lies dry and withered in the grave. The poet, bringing his songs of praise to men, carries drink to the dry (*N*. 3.6-7).

Faced with the possibility of Hades, men sought various miraculous antidotes to death, and created substances and talismans thought to carry with them the promise of unending life. Mythical individuals attempt to take from the gods the possessions which promote their immortal condition, and legendary peoples are often granted death-defying powers and practices. According to Pindar, only one force permits the individual to transcend his own mortality, that of the song the poet creates. The ode naturally assumes the shape of substances invested with death-defeating powers. Nectar and ambrosia were thought a possible source of the gods' immortality, the divine nourishment which replaces meat and grain among the

---

[11] See Eustathius ad *Od*. 6.201 and Onians, op.cit., p.254 on the connection between death and dryness.

Olympians.[12] Pindar describes his poetry as an ambrosial spring of words (*P.* 4.299), a liquid nectar which he dispatches to his laudandus (*O.* 7.7). Honey is nectar's closest equivalent on earth, and in some accounts is a food also favoured by lesser divinities, Muses, Nymphs and Graces.[13] Vedic lore explicitly identifies *soma*, the red or yellow-gold liquid which serves as the source of all life, and banishes death, with *madhu*, honey, [14] and the substance's known powers of conservation make it a potent symbol for continuing life. Pindar's metaphors of his honeyed songs suggest the conserving and immortalising forces that reside in his verse. The sweet food serves as a vehicle for the poet's hope that he may grant a lasting glory to the men and cities that he celebrates and, at *O.* 10.97-9 he writes:

ἐγὼ δὲ συνεφαπτόμενος σπουδᾷ, κλυτὸν ἔθνος
Λοκρῶν ἀμφέπεσον, μέλιτι
εὐάνορα πόλιν καταβρέχων·

> But I, joining in eagerly, embraced the famed race of
> Locrians, drenching in honey the city of fine men.

Here honey, like water, nourishes and irrigates the soil, making it fertile ground for the everlasting growth of fame. Other liquids also carry the promise of immortality, and fantastical springs, fountains and rivers carry antidotes to death. Such springs appear in the Garden of the Hesperides, close by the tree which bears the apples of unending youth, and in the Field of Reeds which Egyptian eschatology devised for the dead. Orphic and Pythagorean philosophies turned the waters of Hades into sources of regeneration and continued life, which provide refreshment for the man thirsty from his distant travels.[15] On one Orphic gold tablet, a fourth-century text from Pharsalos in Thessaly, the dead man is instructed in the geography of the Underworld:

[12] Cf. W.H. Roscher, *Nektar und Ambrosia* (Leipzig, 1883).

[13] Porphyry calls honey the food of the gods in *de antro Nympharum* 16, perhaps an echo of the much earlier description in the Homeric *Hymn to Hermes* of the Thriae who feed on the honeycomb, 'sweet food of the gods' (562). For further discussion of honey see Scheinberg, op.cit., and H. Usener, 'Milch und Honig', *Kleine Schriften* 4 (Leipzig, Berlin, 1918).

[14] *Rig Veda* 8.2.3.

[15] Cf. Vernant, op.cit., p.61f.

In the halls of Hades you will find on the right a spring, with a white cypress beside it. Go nowhere near this spring, but further on you will find cold water running from the Lake of Memory. Above it are guards ... You will tell them the whole truth ... I am dry with thirst, allow me to drink from the spring.[16]

The waters of song which Pindar provides are a far surer means of achieving immortality, and foster the life not only of the individual, but of his family and community. The poet repeatedly contrasts the right and wrong ways towards undying existence. Tales of attempts by Tantalus to take from the gods their nectar and ambrosia (*O.* 1.60f.) and of Bellerophon who sought to attain the Olympian heights (*I.* 7.44-7), serve as negative *exampla* to the victor's own career, and to the *laudandus* who sees in merit and just conduct the correct *pharmakon* to death. Song is a much more enduring drug than medicine can supply, and *P.* 3 is built about the opposing poles of the doctor's temporary powers of healing, and the eternal ones of song. Even Asclepius met with anger from the gods when he wanted to bring a man back from death, using the arts of medicine, not poetry (55f.).

Men also tried to defeat death in more modest ways, surrounding the corpse with rites and iconography designed to suggest the undying existence of some part of the body or soul, and the possibility of its happiness in a future life. Pindar draws on these rites and motifs as a further source of metaphor in his representations of song, and sets its composition and performance within the context of ceremonies enacted on behalf of the dead. The rites of burial serve a double function; they both restore the ritual purity of those who have contact with the miasma of death, and appease the ghost of the dead man which might still linger about the grave or pyre, unwilling to take a final departure.[17] The Greeks propitiated the dead with offerings of food and drink; water jars stood about the grave, holding liquid to satisfy the dead man's thirst, and libations of honey, milk, water and grain were poured out at the tomb. Pindar's songs, which take the shape of these food and liquid gifts,

---

[16] Quoted in Vermeule, op.cit., p.58.
[17] For a useful general account of burial practices and beliefs see D. Kurtz and J. Boardman, *Greek Burial Customs* (London, 1971).

address themselves to the dead as well as the living victors. The poet dispatches a *melikraton*, the milk-and-honey drink specifically designed for those who dwelt in chthonic realms, and could not receive wine (*N.* 3.76-8).[18] While offerings might quiet the souls of the dead, and remove any hostility they felt towards the living, commemorations of a more lasting kind would also serve to create a place for them in men's memory. The athletic competitions which frequently accompanied the burial of heroes were designed to please the individual with imitations of the feats he himself performed, and to stand as recurring reminders of his life and deeds.[19] The Games might be held around the tombs, monuments and cenotaphs which the Greeks erected as lasting testimonials to their dead, and Pindar likewise builds gravestones of his songs, the *stêlê*, (*N.* 4.81), *mnêmê* (*I.* 8.62) and *lithos* (*N.* 8.47) which keep alive the name of the laudandus in future generations.

Commemoration and appeasement both suggest a belief in the continued existence of some part of the individual consciousness, capable of entertaining feelings of pleasure or of grief. If some portion of the man prevailed over death, it was likely to be the soul which might assume a changed and novel shape. Visualisations of this immortal part of the individual form a common motif in funeral iconography, and provide Pindar with an additional source of imagery within the theme of the everlasting life of song. His ode takes on the form which the soul might adopt when it passes from the body of the dead man onto a new existence in some unknown land. A winged creature, sometimes a bird, represents the flight of consciousness, and birds are a standard motif on graves and cenotaphs.[20] The bee also symbolises the rebirth of the soul when the corpse is left behind, and later mythology makes of the honey on which the

---

[18] On the different offerings made to the gods and the dead see S. Eitrem, *Opferritus und Voropfer der Griechen und Römer* (Christiania, 1915), and K. Meuli, 'Griechische Opferbraüche', *Phyllobolia: Festschrift für Peter von der Mühll*, (Basel, 1946) p.185f.

[19] On the possible funeral origins of the Games see K. Meuli, 'Der Ursprung der Olympischen Spiele', *Die Antike* 17 (1941), pp.189-208, and Meuli, *der griechische Agon* (Cologne, 1968).

[20] Kurtz and Boardman, op.cit., pp.135 and 238 for examples of animals on graves.

insect feeds the source of life's renewal.[21] Wings describe the capacity of men for future travel, and permit the soul to leave the immobile body in the grave. Other rites and symbols surrounding death carry notions of a rejuvenation of life, and represent conditions men hope to find in the lands that lie beyond the grave. The leaves and garlands which characterise Pindaric verse also appear in funerary art where they describe the return of fertility in reply to sterile death. Before burial, the corpse might be placed on a bed of leaves, and the early Greeks are said to have favoured evergreens which suggest nature's power of self-renewal.[22] Wreaths decorated the dead man's bier and his house was hung with garlands and sprays of leaves, symbols of new growth and fruitfulness.[23] Significantly, the wreath, both literal and figurative, appears at the moment when Pindar speaks simultaneously of the crowning or flowering of the living and the dead (*I.* 8.62-4).[24]

A further important rite which the living carried out was the performance of the *thrênos*, the lamentation the women of the household sang over the body of the dead. While the victory song expresses joy at success, and the lament serves as an outlet for grief, both are designed to keep a man's name alive in the minds of the participants, and both address the concerns of the living and the dead. Pindar's antithetical style and his particular choice of motifs has much in common with the lament which also builds on contrasting representations of life and death, and the passage between the two. Light and darkness, spring and harvest, water and thirst, the tree and leaf, departure and arrival are all traditional ideas which feature prominently in the dirge.[25]

[21] On the bee as a symbol of regeneration see A.B. Cook, op.cit., and W. Robert Tornow, *De apium mellisque apud veteres significatione et symbolica et mythologica* (Berlin, 1893). In Porphyry's account of the cave of the Nymphs, the unborn souls are called *Melissai*. The author explains that not all souls moving towards generation deserve this title, but only those who 'live justly and who, having performed such things as are acceptable to the gods, will return whence they came' (18). Honey, standing in jars about the cave, provides nourishment for the unborn.

[22] Cumont, op.cit., p.42.

[23] M. Alexiou, *The Ritual Lament in Greek Tradition* (Cambridge, 1974), p.5.

[24] On the symbolic significance of the wreath in this context see remarks on garlands and crowns in J. Duchemin, 'L'iconographie funéraire et l'exégèse Pindarique', *REL* 32 (1954), pp.284-97.

[25] Alexiou, op.cit., p.185f. The author gives examples of the style and structure of both modern and ancient Greek laments.

However, unlike most laments, the ode establishes the opposing poles only to transcend the distance between them; Pindar's poetry is a far-shining ray which permits the light of a man's life to go on unquenched, a stream of water which, unlike the mortal life substance, cannot run dry. In the lament, man flowers in the springtime and is plucked in autumn, but through the cycle which poetry constructs, the dead man's winter is capped by the victor's brilliant springtime bloom. In Pindar's dirges themselves the theme is frequently not the bitterness of mortality, but rather the rewards of the just, rewards which, Pindar's poem intimates, the athlete too will receive.

As he addresses both the living and the dead, Pindar presents the song as an integral part of the rites which join the two. The poem makes the presence of the men of the past a truly living one, summoning them from their resting place to participate in the victor's triumph and to join the audience at the performance of the song. Through metaphor, Pindar describes how his song may actually travel down to Hades, or to the shrines in which the dead heroes reside, quickening their attention. He thus suggests the continuing life of men whose deeds have been celebrated in song, and who derive pleasure from the present day victor's re-enactment of their prowess. The living laudandus is set within the cultic practices observed in honour of the dead, seasonal events which preserve the memory of the individual among those who celebrate the rite. Towards the close of *O*. 1, Pindar describes the funeral sacrifices performed in honour of Pelops, and which are seen as making the dead hero return through the regular celebration of his trial and subsequent reward (90-5). Song stands on a par with cult, and with the festivals which act out rather than speak the praise of gods and heroes. In *N*. 5.36f., the seasonal welcoming of Poseidon serves as a pivot between the tale of Peleus and Pindar's return to his laudandus, establishing clear analogical relations which bring together cult and song.[26]

Metaphors of death paradoxically portray the eternal life of song. Pindar's symbolic representations of his verse collapse distinctions between life and death, and make poetry a power even in the chthonic realms, replacing decay and lack of generation with growth and future motion. He constructs an alternative to the finality of Hades, and to the idyllic lands

[26] Cf. Mullen, op.cit., p.160.

which myth and epic devise. The celebration of a man's name, he suggests, is sufficient to endow him with immortal life as he participates in the undying nature of the word. In speaking of the eternal existence of song, and of the man it praises, Pindar also addresses his own role as poet. Through metaphor, he links the fate of the victor to that of his celebrant, describing how their preservation will be a mutual one. Pindar's intimations of his own lasting life rest on a double surety, his often asserted confidence in the value of his verse, and the actual possibility of textual transmission that the written word holds out.[27]

[27] The notion of the preservation of the text was no mere poetic conceit on Pindar's part. A scholiast remarks that *O.* 7 was inscribed in gold, and dedicated at the temple of Athena on Lindos.

12

Between Myth and Metaphor

Throughout the preceding discussion of metaphor, material has been freely drawn from myth, and myth itself presented as part of the level of extra-verbal figuration the odes include. Myths tell of the gods and of heroes, of the places remote, fantastical and divine which Pindar uses as sources of his metaphors. Although the mythical portions contain less obviously symbolic language than do the other parts of the song, they may themselves be regarded as extended metaphors, drawn out images which contribute to Pindar's thematic and stylistic ends. The myths, whether continuous narrative or brief allusions, carry many of the targets of other Pindaric metaphors, and function through similar devices of polarity, analogy and juxtaposition. This view of myth as metaphor will present another facet of Pindar's use of symbolic representation, and of the poet's departure from a world of ordinary reference into one of greater density of thought and language.

Pindaric myth has been the object of considerable attention as critics and commentators have long sought to resolve the question of its relevance to the victor and poem at large. Some myths show a clear connection with the other material the ode includes; the tale may speak of events closely linked to the victor, his family, ancestry and city or homeland. It may highlight one aspect of his past history or triumphs, evoking battles he has won and the event in which he achieved his victory. At the broader level, myth may illuminate a poem's particular theme, providing a concrete example of a motif that the poet wishes to explore. In the absence of thematic links, Pindar draws together myth and actual circumstances through verbal echoes, using recurrent language and imagery to create an impression of continuity. However, to understand the poet's mythical material at the literal level alone is to mistake both its role in Pindar and the more general nature of myth itself. Myth is analogous to metaphor, a means of speaking of one thing in terms of another. Like metaphor, it does not refer directly to the subject it apparently treats, but has a structure of sense beyond that of explicit expression. Both suggest meanings that lie outside the verbal realm, speaking not through mere 'signs' but through 'symbols'.[1] In structure and in application, myth resembles metaphor, functioning through polarity and analogy, likeness and juxtaposition. Both possess the capacity to dislocate and change normal sequences and expectations, and both may thus articulate that which defies expression in more literal terms. Myth, like metaphor, contributes to the construction of the particular world in which Pindar sets his victors, where poet and athlete mix freely with gods and heroes, and cross the everyday boundaries of space and time.

Pindar's use of myth is highly individual, treating the traditional tale as a flexible device which he may alter, abridge or add to at will. His medium is a fluid one; the Greek myth readily admits the particular application the poet desires, and changes not only according to new interpretations but also with the author's aesthetic design.[2] Mythical and historical time form a continuum in Pindar's odes which, in keeping with the common character of myth, portray time present as an extension of time past.[3] History for Pindar begins with the theogonies, and passes from the acts of creation of the gods to the deeds of foundation of heroes, deeds which find a latter day echo in the activities of the victors and patrons he celebrates. The progression is a linear one, if not measurable in calendar terms. The heroes of myth are frequently the direct descendants of the gods, products of matches between mortal and divine, and present-day victors may trace their lineage back to those legendary figures of the past. The victor re-enacts the deeds of valour of his heroic and immortal ancestors, and the merit which his conduct gives witness to has its roots in the mythical age of which the Games are the surviving relic. Myth can account for the original performance of the feats which Pindar describes,

---

[1] I use these terms according to the distinctions now established between signification, in which a signifier means a signified, and symbolisation, in which a first signified symbolises a second.

[2] The character of Greek mythic material is discussed in Kirk, op.cit., p.172f..

[3] For a view of Pindar's approach to history see G. Huxley, *Pindar's Vision of the Past* (Belfast, 1975), p.23f.

whether carried out by the athlete, singer or tyrant who stands as the contemporary representative of the epic past. It both recalls a Golden Age of prowess and virtue and, to some extent, recreates this past era in present days.[4]

Myth is one of the essential elements of the epinician song, and its immediate purpose is to establish links between the victor and his legendary or divine kin. Like so much of the material in the odes, myth is primarily encomiastic, providing yet another lens which magnifies the worth of the individual laudandus. Like metaphor, and the *eikôn*, illustration, or *parabolê*, comparison, with which the figure was frequently classed, myth is a means of comparative illustration. The legendary hero is a paradigm of excellence, a positive exemplum in *P.* 6 where Pindar draws an explicit parallel between the filial devotion of Thrasybulus, the victor's son, and that of Antilochus who sacrificed his life for his father, Nestor (40f.). The poet's introduction of the myth of Heracles at *N.* 1.33 clearly demonstrates the affinity between the hero and the victor Chromius, both achieving deeds of great prowess. Castor and Iolaus in *I.* 1 have won their legendary renown as actual athletes, and form an obvious parallel to the present-day victor, Herodotus. The negative exemplum serves not merely as a warning but, in accordance with Pindar's wish to place the laudandus at the centre of the praise, a foil for the victor's merit. The tale of Tantalus in the first *Olympian* shows the dangers of excessive ambition, and contrasts the life of the unfortunate thief with that of Pelops and, by implication, the victor. One demonstrates slothful gluttony, overcome by his own excessive good fortune (55-7), while Pelops and Hieron choose a course of active heroism and participation in the Games (95-6). Encomium, not piety or humanitarianism, lies behind the many changes Pindar introduces to his mythical tales, altering their chronology and contents. The acts of violence, spite and childlike rage which both gods and heroes frequently commit would detract from the value of the mythical past as a time of deeds of

---

[4] This conforms in part to Mircea Eliade's theory of the function of myth according to which all myths evoke or actually re-establish a creative era in an attempt to revive some of its unique power. This approach is, however, incompatible with the majority of Greek myths which treat events outside this so-called Golden Age. See M. Eliade, *Myths, Dreams and Mysteries* (New York, 1971).

merit and prowess, and Pindar deliberately omits direct mention of them. He will not compare his athlete with Heracles, the devourer of live oxen, but with the coloniser, explorer and founder of cities and Games. If he comes up against an aspect of his tale of dubious morality, Pindar first protests against it, and then declares that he has nothing to say. At *N*. 5.16f. this device directly contributes to his end of praise as Pindar turns unpropitious material into a foil for subsequent celebration of the victor's heritage. At *O*. 9.30f. reverence again serves poetic ends; Pindar cites Heracles' battles with Poseidon, Apollo and Hades, suggesting a parallel between the hero's feats and those of the family he is called on to praise. When, according to the poet's express design, the exemplum tends towards impiety in its account of men who set themselves up against the gods, he may dismiss the exhausted theme and turn instead to praise of the victor's home.[5]

Through its generation of exempla, both positive and negative, myth furnishes Pindar with a scale of values by which he may measure the men of his day. This coincides with the broader function of myth as a categorical structure which provides a set of familiar points of reference for the evaluation of new concepts and ideas.[6] The purpose of Pindar's verse, like that of myth, is to sanction certain kinds of behaviour, to celebrate what is praiseworthy, and blame what is not. Pindar states his role at *N*. 8.38-9:

ἐγὼ δ' ἀστοῖς ἁδὼν καὶ χθονὶ γυῖα καλύψαι,
αἰνέων αἰνητά, μομφὰν δ' ἐπισπείρων ἀλιτ'ροῖς.

(I pray) to be covered in earth as one who was pleasing to his fellow citizens, who praised what was praiseworthy and spread blame on the evil-doers.

While metaphor builds on the feelings of respect or revulsion which a particular vehicle evokes in the audience, myth may act

---

[5] Cf. Bundy, op.cit., pp.9 and 74.

[6] This is the role ascribed to myth at the beginnings of an 'age of rationalism' by G.S. Kirk, 'Aetiology, ritual, charter: three equivocal terms in the study of myths', *YCS* 22 (1972), p.85f.

out the terms of a moral dilemma or ethical choice. Pindar's mythical characters, most notably Ajax, Achilles and Pelops, are men who must face the decision between a life of ease and safety at home, and one of toil and danger in remote places. Like that of the victor in *O.* 12, their choice is sanctioned by the Pindaric scale of values where the life of the athlete is set above all others. Struggle, victory and subsequent renown make up the moral pattern to which the lives of all men of virtue should conform. Myth, like metaphor, generates its own gnomic material, carrying the moral message which the epinician involves.

In entering on the realm of values, myth, like metaphor, extends its scope beyond the immediate victory which the poem celebrates. Victory has implications for all men, and myth and metaphor generalise its significance by introducing themes which relate to common concerns. Thus myth demonstrates how success comes only at the price of toil and struggle, illustrating this recurrent idea with the figure of Perseus who, in *P.* 12, must perform many labours before winning his just deserts. Envy is a constant threat to the victor and to any man who has achieved uncommon success, and forms the central motif of the Ajax tale in *N.* 8.[7] The hero's suicide follows on Pindar's general reflection on the nature of an emotion which *haptetai d' eslôn aei, cheironessi d' ouk erizei*, always fastens on the best of men but does not quarrel with the wicked (22). Many hostile forces threaten men even after they have won glory with their toil and effort, and poetry alone has the capacity to dispel the misrepresentation that hostile elements might promote. The theme of poetic truth is carried in the myth of Ajax and Neoptolemus in *N.* 7, where both heroes receive praise in verse as a reward for their exertions and eventual deaths; song holds a primacy of place in the life of the victor, and relates a tale which will itself become the stuff of myth. Poetry alone can recompense the athlete for his pains, and its power to soothe and heal suggests the myth of Asclepius in *P.* 3, a tale of medical remedies. While medicine may merely postpone a man's inevitable death, song can preserve his name everlastingly. The myth of the Hyperboreans in *P.* 10 likewise visualises the theme of perpetual celebration, the state of song, dance and revelry

---

[7] For a detailed discussion of the motif see A. Köhnken, *Die Funktion des Mythas bei Pindar* (Berlin, 1971), p.34f.

which Pindar creates through his verse.[8]

In its treatment of abstract themes, myth may function as little more than symbol, divorced from its usual context. Pindar can rely on his audience's familiarity with the tales he draws on, and may use a single event for symbolic representation. The Pillars of Heracles provide one example of myth 'symbolised'; the legendary hero's voyage to Gades, where he subdued the hound of Geryones, represents the limits of mortal endeavour beyond which no man may pass. Through mention of the landmark the hero established on his voyage, Pindar signals that the laudandus has achieved the high point of human worth. Another mythical symbol which serves to illustrate a more general point than its traditional context suggests is Typhon. The monster, soothed by the music played by Cadmus on his flute, is tricked into allowing Zeus to regain the thunderbolt which he had stolen.[9] In Pindar he appears as an example of the power of song to touch even the most savage of tempers in its preservation of a universal harmony (*P.* 1.13f.).

Myth as symbol appears even outside the actual mythical narrative most odes include, and passes beyond the formal limits which the tale sets down. Pindar weaves it into the entire fabric of the poem, passing from myth to metaphor in his transition from one subject or theme to the next. Both devices contribute to the structure of the ode, the impression of continuity which the poet seeks, as metaphor is made to suggest myth, and myth metaphor. The maritime metaphors of *P.* 10 coincide with the myth of Perseus' voyage to the land of the Hyperboreans, a tale which Pindar introduces with the image of the limits which mortals cannot cross (27-30). Myth and metaphor are intertwined in *N.* 7 where the fatal journey of Ajax suggests the general symbol of the wave of Hades (31). The interplay between the elements frequently depends on both thematic and verbal repetitions; in *N.* 8, the metaphor of envy which fastens upon noble men returns in the myth some few lines later when the same tenacious emotion

---

[8] Köhnken has argued that the description of the Hyperboreans is intended to illustrate the delights offered by poetry, and serves as an image of immortality through song, Köhnken, op.cit., p.83.

[9] One extensive account of the myth of Typhon may be found in the first two books of Nonnus' *Dionysiaka*.

Τελαμῶνος δάψεν υἱόν,
φασγάνῳ ἀμφικυλίσαις.

(23)¹⁰

devoured the son of Telamon, rolling him about his sword.

Through the combination of myth and metaphor, Pindar smoothes over the joins between the different portions of his verse, and makes the transition virtually imperceptible, embedded in the mythical narrative itself. At *P.* 9.67 the poet prepares to bring his account of the marriage between Apollo and Cyrene to a close, and signals his intention with the statement:

ὠκεῖα δ' ἐπειγομένων ἤδη θεῶν
πρᾶξις ὁδοί τε βραχεῖαι.

Accomplishment is swift when the gods are already making haste, and the paths short.

The god's speed of accomplishment parallels the poet's own activity as he uses a conventional device for concluding one element of the ode and passing to another.¹¹ The use of the mythical symbol performs a parallel function at *I.* 1.13 where Pindar's reference to Heracles' western travels provides a stopping point for the opening unit of the song. Beyond Gadeira neither the laudandus nor laudator may go. In promoting the structure of the verse, myth and metaphor act in complementary relationship, and the natural affinity between the two devices allows the poem to move from one to the other without any obvious break in sense.

The affinity that myth and metaphor share includes not only their role within the odes, but their actual composition. Myth acts through comparison and juxtaposition, through the bringing together of the same disparate spheres that metaphor draws on. It involves the mingling of mythical and real material, lending significance to the latter through the perspective the former provides. To use terms proper to metaphor, the laudandus or

---

¹⁰ For a close analysis of the verbal interaction within this metaphor see Silk, op.cit., p.165.
¹¹ Cf. Bundy, op.cit., p.2.

poetic theme acts as the tenor of the mythical narrative, the traditional tale itself as the vehicle. Myth as positive exemplum or paradigm builds on the likeness between the hero and athlete, while myth as negative exemplum displays relevant unlikeness, a contrast which serves to magnify the victor's worth. Like metaphor, myth may build on a pre-existing likeness in its suggestion of novel applications and relations of meaning. The Orestes' myth in *P.* 11 derives its formal relevance from the fact that the victory occurred at Delphi, and that the god most closely associated with the shrine, Apollo, played a critical part in the legendary hero's fortunes. The actual significance of the tale lies in the contrast it promotes between the troubled life of Orestes, and his conflict with his family, and the life of the athlete, marked by civic devotion and loyalty to family and friends.[12] A single myth may encompass both similarity and difference, analogous to the epiphoric and diaphoric metaphor. The Hyperboreans in *P.* 10 enjoy an existence which mirrors that of the athlete in the midst of the celebration of his triumph. However, while the delight that success grants to mortal men is of a brief duration, the Hyperboreans enjoy enternal pleasure, free from all sickness and old age (41-4). Contrast and comparison join the myth to actuality, and also characterise the construction of Pindaric myth itself. Pindar may select two tales to illustrate related concerns, allowing one to complement the other and cast a further light on the poetic theme. In *N.* 7, the myth of Neoptolemus reinforces and broadens the implications of the Ajax tale which it closely follows. Both treat the general theme of deeds of prowess, death and posthumous renown, but while Ajax takes his own life, Neoptolemus is killed in a fight. The myths of Tantalus and Pelops in the first *Olympian* stand in sharp contrast to one another, a contrast which Pindar underlines with his use of repeated linguistic motifs. While Tantalus is unable to 'digest' his own excess of good fortune, Pelops refuses to 'boil away' a vain old age (83). Pindar's mythical narrations show the same fondness for contrast and antithesis as his metaphors which play on shifts between light and dark, tempest and calm, fertility and barrenness. The tale of Iamos, in Pindar's account, follows the hero from his birth

---

[12] David Young argues for the relevance of Orestes' tale as a foil for the life of the athlete. Young, op.cit., p.3f.

among the gold and purple flowers to his encounter with Poseidon in the black of night, symbolic of the dangers which the solitary existence of a hero must include. The myth of Ajax in *N*. 8 is constructed about the poles of the *esloi*, good, and the *cheirones*, evil, the illustrious and the obscure (22f.). Both myth and metaphor achieve their end through combining elements in diverse ways, always suggesting a variety of relations in the reality they contemplate. While the arrangement of elements in metaphor is immediately apparent, myth progresses in more leisurely ways, giving drawn out representation to the networks it discovers.

A similarity in patterns of thought and apprehension underlies both devices, and accounts for their affinities. Myth parallels metaphor in two fundamental ways, in how it is used and in its relation to external events. A tale is neither bound to any particular text nor to a pragmatic reality. Every tale or *muthos*, like every metaphor, has an element of deliberate *poiêsis*, of fiction, which sets it and the *logos* quite apart. To use *logos* consists of assembling single bits of fact and evidence while myth makes no pretence of external verifiability. The myth-maker claims no responsibility for his tale, nor can he point back to any original, true version.[13] The *muthos/logos* division is a fundamental one in Greek thought. It may be seen, in some sense, as corresponding to differences between speech as symbolisation and speech as signification, the first irreducible to logical account, the second satisfying the laws of demonstration. Just as metaphor treats words as more than the simple conveyors of external objects and ideas, so mythical language has a structure of sense contained within the discrete expression itself. Mythical, like metaphoric speech, is characteristically dense, made up of units which each possesses its own significance beyond its immediate context, sustaining several meanings simultaneously. Both myth and metaphor are difficult to interpret on account of the multiple levels of meaning they include. Both display secondary reference since representation, which is patently symbolic, always creates a gap between sign and sense. The figurative character of myth is even more absolute than that of metaphor; while metaphor can lose its

[13] On the *muthos/logos* distinction see W. Burkert, *Structure and History in Greek Mythology and Ritual* (Berkeley and Los Angeles, 1979), p.3. Further bibliography is given in the author's n.14.

symbolic nature, and become the only current designation for a particular object, myth always remains incompatible with the world 'out there', guarding its distance from what it apparently narrates.

Throughout Greek accounts, myth is viewed in one of two different ways; either it expresses in indirect or allegorical form the same truth which the *logos* explicitly conveys, or it addresses that which lies outside the demonstrable truth, and has no place within logical discourse.[14] The first view may be seen as matching the ancient approach to metaphor; there it was but a device of style, a means of lending variety to literal speech. Both myth and metaphor were favoured rhetorical tricks, adding interest and colour to the orator's delivery. Neither was a vital part of language which covered every contingency with its literal terms. The second view of myth approximates the modern approach to metaphor, which regards it as a way of expressing what otherwise cannot be articulated. Myth, with its treatment of gods and supernatural creatures, of fantastical deeds and faraway places, deals even more explicitly than metaphor with the realm of imagination, perceived by the ancients as manifestly 'untrue'. The place of myth lies somewhere between the two views, bringing fantasy and reality into closer connection and suggesting mythical levels in the real, and real levels in myth. It does not necessarily speak of 'something else' but of the very thing which, though actual, cannot be said in any other fashion.

Myth appears in many of the same contexts as metaphor, where language must take in and give expression to the unfamiliar, remote or intangible. One theory of the function of myth points to its role in allegorising natural events, giving names, characters and histories to the elements which men could not explain in other fashions.[15] This parallels the use of metaphor to animate and anthropomorphise, to transfer the language of men and animals to natural phenomena. Both myth and metaphor pass beyond this simple exchange and through personification suggest new relationships not immediately

---

[14] A general discussion of the Greek attitude towards myth may be found in J.-P. Vernant, *Mythe et société en Grèce ancienne* (Paris, 1979), p.195f.
[15] The theory that all myths are nature myths began in Germany, but gained many followers in England, most notably Max Müller.

evident in the natural forces viewed more directly. The representation of the earth and sky as the married couple Gaia and Ouranos casts new light on the connections between moisture, the earth and fertile life. The aetiological theory of myth suggests that its function is to explain, to give account for what is striking or incomprehensible.[16] Again metaphor plays an analogous role, acting as a source of description for events which lie outside the bounds of human reasoning. Myth can interpret the unknown, populating unexplored areas with creatures fantastical and divine. The pre-established structure of the myth allows it to take in new phenomena; whenever the Greeks, in the course of their colonising expeditions, encountered people who effectively resisted their domination, and boasted a culture equal to that of the Greeks themselves, they were dubbed 'Trojans', Trojan allies or offspring. Thus, in the *Iliad*, Phrygians and Lydians both fight for Troy.[17] Myth performs a more complex aetiological function when it expresses abstract or metaphysical concepts. Plato makes use of myth to explain both things which lie beyond and those that fall short of strictly philosophical language, in his descriptions of the working of the soul, and his account of the concepts of destiny and immortality, of the birth of the world. These areas likewise attract metaphorical expressions. Myth and metaphor not only treat the intangible, but can find a means of illuminating abstract problems at both narrative and analytical levels, through terms at once traditional and symbolic. The Prometheus tale illustrates a mythical treatment of an ethical problem; the myth does not merely establish a precedent for the division of sacrificial meats but, through Prometheus' trickery and Zeus' retaliation, acts out the debate of a moral issue. Human experience is frequently paradoxical, contradictory, and myth and metaphor can discover ways if not to resolve, at least to express its multiple facets. The myth of Pandora portrays in concrete form the ambivalent relation between the sexes, man's view of woman as a necessary ill. A single myth often represents two antithetical impulses or desires, showing reverence with impiety, nobility with violence. The figure of Heracles is compounded of many

---

[16] The aetiological theory of myth was first advanced by A. Lang, and developed in his *Myth, Ritual and Religion* (London, 1887).

[17] Cf. Burkert, op.cit., p.25.

contradictory modes of behaviour; the hero is at once founder,
coloniser and saviour, and the practitioner of deeds of senseless
cruelty. Many of the athletes elevated to hero status in local cult
display the same rapid shifts between virtue and violence,[18]
while the mythical Centaurs act as visualisations of the twin
impulses men may know. According to the theory of
Lévi-Strauss, the polar nature of mythical material is the result
of the structure of the human mind, the ultimate source of
mythical invention. One of the main features of the mind is its
binary character which causes it to divide experience for the
purposes of understanding into sets of opposites. Myth
constructs pseudo-logical categories which may resolve or
mitigate the polarities which the human brain perceives,
enabling men to accept, if not explain, contradictory elements in
their environment.[19] Something of the same could be said of
metaphor, a device which brings into a composite expression
apparently antithetical objects and ideas, neither resolving nor
dissolving their unlikeness, but holding both in one.

The interplay of several levels of meaning characterises both
myth and metaphor. Interaction features in both, illustrating
real situations through the perspective of imaginary ones. Myth
may break down the normal divisions between reality and
fantasy by illuminating actual experience through the co-
presence of an unfamiliar context, initially quite distinct. The
fresh insight that it grants validates the use of the symbolic.
Myth and metaphor involve the linking of the literal with the
figurative levels of speech and experience. They can create novel
alignments between real and imaginary situations despite the
lack of overt correspondence. Abstraction is another feature
which belongs to myth as well as metaphor; the poet may take
from a particular object or situation the significance he wishes,
rejecting what is not pertinent to the target of the metaphor or
tale. The myth-maker abstracts the underlying structure of
sense from the narrative while altering the surrounding elements
at will. Each myth holds a different significance for the
individual author which he reveals through selecting the

[18] On the capacity of the athlete for acts both worthy and evil, see Fontenrose,
op.cit.

[19] Lévi-Strauss outlines his theory in *Structural Anthropology* (Harmondsworth and New York, 1976).

particular facets he requires. The structure of sense in myth, like the target of the metaphor, may change. When retold in a different age or situation, different features of the myth emerge and a new balance is struck between its variables. Neither myth nor metaphor has an original, 'true' meaning, but both are the products of their context, usage and the understanding speaker and listener bring. Flexibility is a vital attribute of these devices which aim to keep the sign system fluid and changing through their generalising powers, and to provide a context by analogy always capable of transformation. The notion of centres of expansion and attraction proper to metaphor is also useful in considering the change that the individual myth may undergo, according to the age and culture. Each society has its own concerns, dictated by its environment and civilisation. Certain features of myth may be closely linked with recognisable cultural strata, such as the prominent role of animals in the tales of a hunting society. As the society progresses, concerns may change and myth develop to meet the new situations. Traditional tales are thus attracted to areas of collective importance while the historical, geographical and social circumstances of the group provide the raw material on which the mythical imagination works.

It is in their appeal to the imagination that myth and metaphor complement one another. Both address not the audience's intellect, but its intuitions, emotions and feelings. Both suspend everyday boundaries of sense and allow the listener to enter a realm where any object can assume a multiplicity of shapes, any word infinite meaning. Myth, like metaphor, ignores the normal chronological and spatial divisions, and the mythical subject may be part of the past, present and future, a dweller in both the real and fantastical world. Myth gives concrete form to some of the combinations that metaphor devises, realising its symbolic representations in the shape of tales which act out the interplay between reality and figuration.

Epilogue

In an earlier chapter, metaphor was examined in terms of its contribution to Pindar's presentation of the subject matter of his song. It was seen as an essential device for praise of the poem's patron, and as a means of structuring the encomiastic material the poet might include. Metaphor also provides a model for the behaviour of the other great term in Pindaric verse, poetry itself. It alone may represent the poetic process, the links it builds between word and deed, laudator and laudandus. Through the distinctive discourse metaphor generates, it discovers the final essence of their unity, and points to the true nature of victory-in-song. Metaphor achieves its end through its capacity to function in two referential fields at once, joining the familiar field of established meaning with the unfamiliar field for which there is no external characterisation, and which stands complete within itself. It is this field which houses the forces which make the Pindaric ode a living, lasting thing.

In order to reach the second field, language must divest itself of its function of direct description. This is the role of the metaphor within poetic discourse where it first destroys the literal level, and then creates new meaning. Metaphor arises from a blockage in literal, inadequate interpretation, exploiting the gap between words and objects, sense and reference, and splintering the illusory bond between name and thing. From this wreckage a more fundamental mode of reference emerges, one which lays the way for a new, more adequate interpretation. Like 'poeticalness' itself, metaphor is not 'a supplementation of discourse, but a total re-evaluation of discourse and of all its components whatsoever'.[1] The breakdown of literal levels of meaning sets us on the road to rediscovery and redescription,

---

[1] R. Jakobson, 'Closing statements: linguistics and poetics', in T.A. Sebeok, (ed.), *Style in Language* (Cambridge, Mass., 1960), p.377.

allowing poet and audience both to step back from a world of ordinary reference where words function as signs, to one of symbols, where words become significant in themselves. This symbolic language is notoriously dense, making words into a more substantial matter which does not merely represent, but expresses. Such opaque discourse replaces denotation with connotation, the hallmark of metaphoric speech.

This language is ideally suited to Pindar's purpose, and to the many transformations which the poetic medium works on the material of the song. While an abstract model of metaphor suggests its mode of operation, the particular images Pindar selects provide actual representations of the transition of language into solid matter which simultaneously imitates, creates and conserves. The poetic process is one of imitation and recall; Pindar holds his mirror up to nature through the agency of the Muses, the goddesses who 'love to remember'. Metaphors of craftsmanship describe the creative act that the poet undertakes, fixing together the various materials that lie about, while floral and plant symbols portray the song as an autonomous thing, creator and created both. The same treasure house that the poet constructs with his words, that forms a new composite beneath the poet's crafting hands, stands as a firm edifice which will permanently preserve his song. In conserving, poetry also makes manifest, and the porch that Pindar builds is a far-shining one. Symbols of light describe how the poet illuminates the essence and the inner workings of the material he draws into his realm, and poetic radiance shines most brightly when he realises the true account of his subject matter and makes tangible and luminous the character of victory and of song. The poet is the individual who best understands the nature of the matter he describes, and who guides other men towards an appreciation of its character. Two other features of poetic language receive visualisation in Pindaric metaphor; participation and mediation. Poetic discourse is participation, the discovery of the relations between things, and of the proximity between them which enables the poet to fuse their discrete identities, and to use one as a means of speaking of the other. Mutual exchange belongs to Pindar's images of birds, beasts and humankind, to his portrayal of the mingling of gods and men when the immortals join in festal revelry and the Muses leave the

Helicon heights to participate in the earthly *kômos*.[2] Mediation is another vital function of poetic speech which is designed to interact between man and the external world, between man and man and within a man himself. It forges passages between areas that normally stand distinct, travelling between literal and figurative meanings, between identity and diference. Through images of the path of land and sea, of flight and voyage, Pindar represents his song belonging to the worlds of gods and men, past and future, life and death.

The fusion of the laudandus with this dense poetic language has a particular result, one which again metaphor alone may express. Pindar's aim with regard to his victor is to make the individual, momentary achievement stand as an idealised representation of success for all time. To effect his transformation, the poet needs a language which itself approximates these conditions of atemporality and ideal form. Poetic discourse tends back towards an idealised speech, that which existed before the split between word and object, sense and reference, when every name stood not merely as an imitation but as an absolute and total realisation of the thing it named, unchanging with time. The vision of words which manifest the essence of the thing they speak belongs to the mythical era and Golden Age in whose context Pindar places himself and his subject, permitting both to exist in harmony with gods, heroes and nature. Poetry and victory both seek expression in the conditions which exist when all things participate in a Platonic world of fundamental being. Pindar's representation of the victory-in-song is no sequential, discursive account, but a discovery of the proximity of all things, a gathering up of all the dispersed forms which belong within the scope of the matter he describes.[3]

The new composite or unity which Pindar creates naturally involves the presence of the divine, the force which finally permits the mingling of the praiser and the praised. Through

---

[2] The festal procession, evoked in literal and figurative form in Pindar's odes, will later be seen as a symbol for an ontological homecoming, man's return to a natural truth. See particularly Heidegger's readings of Hölderlin in M. Heidegger, *Erläuterungen zu Hölderlins Dichtung* 4th ed. (Frankfurt, 1971).

[3] This corresponds to Heidegger's account of true speaking as a harvesting, collecting and ingathering of the dispersed vestiges of being. Cf. 'Letter on Humanism', trans. Edgar Lohner, in W. Barrett and H.D. Aiken (eds), *Philosophy in the Twentieth Century 3* (New York, 1962).

metaphor, Pindar can express the element of divinity that unquestionably resides in both poetry and the particular glory of the patron in song. Poetry is itself a gift of the gods, and human success, in Pindar's conventional religious view, comes only as a favour from the immortals. The moment of triumph and the moment of poetic initiation are both epiphanies, the appearance of the gods on earth. The poem carries the divine in more permanent form. It serves as an icon in a double sense, at once a dense material which captures meaning in itself, and the expression of the presence of some other force which moves and works through it.[4] The metaphors in poetry can address the gods, suggesting a model for their own mode of operation within the lives of athletes and poets. Poetic discourse speaks at once of what it makes manifest, and what it hides, the qualities of covertness and exhibition which simultaneously exist within the great work of art. The metaphor itself may be understood as a representation of the relation the visible bears to the invisible as it describes the relation of the laudator and laudandus to the manifest yet intangible divine forces that work through it. The divine must move through the poet's language and the athlete's act in order for one to give lasting form to the other in the close coincidence between the word and deed. The relationship between poetic discourse and the divine is a circular one; metaphor presents man's relation to the divine through the media in which the divine manifests itself to man, song and success.

Pindar's language addresses the gods in both direct and indirect ways, through actual invocations and through the oblique references contained in metaphor. He measures man's relation to these figures in his appropriation of the symbols of their divinity, evoking the Olympian realms in his images of gold, eternal light, festivities and dance which recreate the existence of the gods on earth. Their possessions, chariots, bows and wings, feature in Pindar's descriptions of the poetic task, and in his account of the moment of success which the victor enjoys. He speaks of mythical figures of the past who stood in particularly close proximity to the gods by virtue of their birth or deeds, and sets himself within the tradition of the ancient bards who served as the stewards of the Muses, and provided mortal

---

[4] On the 'iconicity' of the poem see Ricoeur, op.cit., p.255.

counterparts to the goddesses who sang the undying glory of the Olympian gods. The ideal speech which Pindaric metaphor approximates, which would make clear the links between all things, also expresses the ultimate bond which links mortal men and objects to the divine.

The poet's own relation to the Olympian realms is a complex one. In searching for a language which will express his particular powers of perceiving the connections between all things, the poet appropriates what is unique to the gods. He is their self-declared representative on earth, the individual who not only stands between men and gods but claims divine powers. In conferring undying life on his laudandus, and striving after personal immortality for himself, the poet rivals the ability of the gods who possess unending existence by nature. Pindar is careful to preserve a reverent attitude to the immortals, involving them in his creative acts through direct prayers and indirect address. His repeated appeals, however, serve both as invocations and implicit provocations, challenging the gods through imitation of their powers. Metaphor stands as the ultimate audacity the poet commits, seeking to establish an axis of relation between the earth and sky, a ladder which the poet and his subjects may travel with or without divine consent. Through his imagery, his symbolic presentation of his arts of music, song and dance, Pindar not only imitates a higher harmony, but intimates the possibility of its existence among men, recreating such conditions as existed before gods and men went on their separate ways. In illuminating the better world the gods enjoy, which normally remains hidden to mortal men, Pindar can meet the gods on their own ground.

It is metaphor which leads the way towards and prepares this special ground, the place where poets encounter their divine counterparts, and heroes mix with present-day victors. It is a ground where pre-objective language prevails, where words and men can realise their potential being. The Pindaric ode articulates and preserves the experience which places a man in speech and invests the speech with life; it sets laudator and laudandus both within the medium of poetic discourse, and discovers in poetry the essential life force which will permit it to grow and move through all time.

Bibliography

Alexiou, M. *The Ritual Lament in Greek Tradition.* Cambridge, 1974.

Annas, J. 'Knowledge and Language: the *Theaetetus* and the *Cratylus*', in Schofield, M. and Nussbaum, M., *Language and Logos.* Cambridge, 1982, pp.95-114.

Aymard, A. 'Hiérarchie du travail et autarcie individuelle dans la Grèce archaïque', *Etudes d'Histoire Ancienne.* Paris, 1967, pp.316-33.

Beardsley, M.C. *Aesthetics.* Repr. Indianapolis, Cambridge, 1981.

Becker, O. Das Bild des Weges und verwandte Vorstellungen im frühgriechischen Denken. *Hermes Einzelschriften* 4. Berlin, 1937.

Benveniste, E. *Problèmes de linguistique générale.* Paris, 1966.

Bernardini, P.A. ' "L'aquila tebana" vola ancora', *QUCC* 26 (1977), pp.121-6.

Black, M. 'More about metaphor', in Ortony, A. (ed.), *Metaphor and Thought.* Cambridge, 1979, pp.19-34.

Bollack, J. 'L'or des rois: le mythe dans la Deuxième Olympique', *RPh* 37 (1963), pp.234-54.

Borthwick, E. 'Zoologica Pindarica', *CQ* n.s. 26 (1976), pp.198-205.

Bowra, C.M. *Pindar.* Oxford, 1964.

Boyancé, P. *Le Culte des Muses chez les philosophes grecs.* Paris, 1937.

Bultmann, R. 'Zur Geschichte der Lichtsymbolik im Altertum', *Philologus* 97 (1948), pp.1-36.

Bundy, E.L. 'Studia Pindarica I & II', *University of California Publications in Classical Philology* 18 (1962), pp.1-34, 34-52.

Burckhardt, J. *Griechische Kulturgeschichte* vol. 1. Berlin 1898-1902.

Burford, A. *Craftsmen in Greek and Roman Society.* London, 1972.

Burkert, W. 'Krekropidensage und Arrephoria', *Hermes* 94 (1966), pp.1-25.

Burkert, W. *Griechische Religion der archaischen und klassischen Epoche.* Stuttgart, 1977.

Burkert, W. *Structure and History in Greek Mythology and Ritual.* Berkeley and Los Angeles, 1979.

Burton, R.W.B. *Pindar's Pythian Odes.* Oxford, 1962.

Carne-Ross, D.S. 'Weaving with points of gold: Pindar's *Sixth Olympian*', *Arion* n.s. 3/1 (1976), pp.5-44.

Chadwick, H.M. and N.K. *The Growth of Literature* vol.1. Cambridge, 1932.

Chantraine, P. *Dictionnaire étymologique de la langue grecque*. Paris, 1974.

Coffey, M. 'The function of the Homeric simile', *AJPh* 78 (1957), pp.113-32.

Cornford, F.M. *Principium Sapientiae: A study of the Origins of Greek Philosophical Thought*. Cambridge, 1952.

Cook, A.B. 'The bee in Greek mythology', *JHS* 15 (1895), pp.1-24.

Crotty, K. *Song and Action*. Baltimore and London, 1982.

Cumont, F. *Lux Perpetua*. Paris, 1949.

Detienne, M. and Vernant, J.-P. *Les Ruses de l'intelligence: la métis des grecs*. Paris, 1974.

Detienne, M. *Les Maîtres de vérité dans la grèce archaïque*. Paris, 1967.

Detienne, M. 'Between beasts and gods', in Gordon, R.L. (ed.), *Myth, Religion and Society*. Cambridge, 1981, pp.215-28.

Detienne, M. 'The sea crow', in Gordon, R.L. (ed.), *Myth, Religion and Society*. Cambridge, 1981, pp.16-42.

Dickie, M. 'On the meaning of *ephêmeros*', *Illinois Classical Studies* I (1975), pp.7-14.

Dieterich, A. *Nekyia*. Leipzig, 1893.

Dodds, E.R. *Euripides' Bacchae with Introduction and Commentary*. Oxford, 1944.

Dodds, E.R. *The Greeks and the Irrational*. Berkeley and Los Angeles, 1951.

Dornseiff, F. *Pindars Stil*. Berlin, 1921.

Duchemin, J. 'Essai sur le symbolisme Pindarique: or, lumière et couleurs', *REG* 65 (1952), pp.46-58.

Duchemin, J. 'L'iconographie funéraire et l'exégèse Pindarique', *REL* 32 (1954), pp.284-97.

Duchemin, J. *Pindare, poète et prophète*. Paris, 1955.

Eitrem, S. *Opferritus und Voropfer der Griechen und Römer*. Christiania, 1915.

Eliade, M. *Myths, Dreams and Mysteries*. New York, 1961.

Elliger, W. *Die Darstellung der Landschaft in der griechischen Dichtung*. Berlin, New York, 1975.

Farnell, L.R. *The Cults of the Greek States*, vol.5. Oxford, 1909.

Farnell, L.R. *The Works of Pindar*, 2 vols. London, 1932.

Finley, M.I. and Pleket, H.W. *The Olympic Games: The First Thousand Years*. London, 1976.

Fontanier, P. *Les Figures du discours*. Repr. Paris, 1968.

Fontenrose, J. 'The hero as athlete', *California Studies in Classical Antiquity* I (1968), pp.73-104.

Fowler, B. 'Imagery of the *Prometheus Bound*', *AJPh* 78 (1957), pp.173-184.

Fränkel, H. *Dichtung und Philosophie des frühen Griechentums*, 2nd ed. Munich, 1962.

Frege, G. 'On sense and reference', in *Philosophical Writings of Gottlob Frege*, trans. Max Black and Peter Geech. Oxford, 1952.

Frontisi-Ducroux, F. *Dédale: mythologie de l'artisan en Grèce ancienne*. Paris, 1975.

Frye, N. *The Educated Imagination*. Toronto, 1963.

Gardiner, E.N. *Greek Athletic Sports and Festivals*. London, 1910.

Gardiner, E.N. 'The alleged kingship of the Olympic victor', *BSA* 22 (1916-1919), pp.85-106.

Gatz, B. *Weltalter, goldene Zeit und sinnverwandte Vorstellungen*. Hildesheim, 1967.

Gerber, D. *Pindar's Olympian I: A Commentary*. Toronto, 1982.

Gernet, L. 'Jeux et droits (remarques sur le XXIIIe chant de l'*Iliade*)' in *Droit et société dans la Grèce antique*. Paris, 1955, pp.9-18.

Gernet, L. *Anthropologie de la Grèce antique*. Paris, 1968.

Gildersleeve, Basil L. *Pindar: The Olympian and Pythian Odes*. New York, 1885.

Gordon, R.L. (ed.) *Myth, Religion and Society*. Cambridge, 1981.

Gundert, F. *Pindar und sein Dichterberuf*. Frankfurt, 1935.

Hamilton, R. *Epinikion: General Form in the Odes of Pindar*. The Hague, Paris, 1974.

Harris, H.A. *Greek Athletes and Athletics*. London, 1964.

Heidegger, M. 'Letter on Humanism', in Barrett, W. and Aiken, H.D. (eds), *Philosophy in the Twentieth Century 3*, New York, 1962.

Heidegger, M. *Erläuterungen zu Hölderlins Dichtung*, 4th ed. Frankfurt, 1971.

Heidegger, M. *On the Way to Language*, trans. Peter D. Hertz. New York, 1971.

Henle, P. (ed.) *Language, Thought and Culture*. Ann Arbor, 1958.

Homberg, U. *Der Baum des Lebens*. Helsinki, 1922.

Huxley, G. *Pindar's Vision of the Past*. Belfast, 1975.

Jaeger, W. *Paideia*, trans. G. Highet. Oxford, 1939-1945.

Jakobson, R. 'Two aspects of language and two types of aphasic disturbances', in Jakobson, R. and Hallé, M., *The Fundamentals of Language*. The Hague, 1956.

Jakobson, R. 'Closing statements: linguistics and poetics', in Sebeok, T.A. (ed.), *Style in Language*. Cambridge, Mass., 1960, pp.350-377.

Kambylis, A. *Die Dichterweihe und ihre Symbolik*. Heidelberg, 1965.

Keller, O. *Die Antike Tierwelt*, 2 vols. Leipzig, 1909-1913.

Kennedy, G. *The Art of Persuasion in Greece*. Princeton, 1963.

Kennedy, G. *Classical Rhetoric*. London, 1980.

Kirk, G.S. *Myth: Its Meaning and Functions in Ancient and Other Cultures*. Berkeley and Los Angeles, 1970.

Kirk, G.S. 'Aetiology, ritual, charter: three equivocal terms in the study of myths', *YCS* 22 (1972), pp.83-102.

Köhnken, A. *Die Funktion des Mythos bei Pindar*. Berlin, 1971.

Konrad, H. *Etude sur la métaphore*. Vrin, 1959.

Kurtz, D. and Boardman J. *Greek Burial Customs*. London, 1971.

Lang, A. *Myth, Ritual and Religion*. London, 1887.

Lebeck, A. *The Oresteia: A Study in Language and Structure*. Washington D.C., 1971.

Lefkowitz, M. 'Tô kai egô: the first person in Pindar', *HSCP* 67 (1965), pp.177-253.

Leftkowitz, M. 'Bacchylides *Ode 5*: imitation and originality', *HSCP* 73 (1969), pp.45-96.

Lefkowitz, M. *The Victory Ode: An Introduction*. New Jersey, 1976.

Lefkowitz, M. 'Pindar's *Nemean XI*, *JHS* 159 (1979), pp.49-56.

Lesky, A. *Thalatta: der Weg der Griechen zum Meer* (Vienna, 1947).

Lévi-Strauss, C. *Structural Anthropology*. Harmondsworth and New York, 1968-1973.

Lloyd, G.E.R. *Polarity and Analogy*. Cambridge, 1966.

Lloyd-Jones, H. 'A problem in the Tebtunis *Inachus*-Fragment', *CR* n.s. 15 (1965), pp.241-3.

Lloyd-Jones, H. 'Modern interpretation of Pindar. The *2nd Pythian* and *7th Nemean Odes*', *JHS* 93 (1973), pp.109-37.

Lloyd-Jones, H. *Females of the Species*. London, 1975.

Lloyd-Jones, H. 'Pindar', *PBA* 68 (1982), pp.139-63.

McCall, M. *Ancient Rhetorical Theories of Simile and Comparison*. Cambridge, Mass., 1969.

McDermott, W.C. 'The ape in Greek literature', *TAPA* 66 (1935), pp.165-76.

McEvilley, T. 'Sapphic imagery and Fragment 96', *Hermes* 101 (1973), pp.257-78.

Maehler, H. *Die Auffassung des Dichterberufs im frühen Griechentum bis zur Zeit Pindars*. Göttingen, 1963.

Majno, G. *The Healing Hand: Man and Wound in the Ancient World*. Cambridge, Mass., 1975.

Martin, J. and Harré, R. 'Metaphor in science', in Miall, D.S. (ed.), *Metaphor: Problems and Perspectives*. Brighton, 1982, pp.89-105.

Meuli, K. 'Scythica', *Hermes* 70 (1935), pp.121-76.

Meuli, K. 'Der Ursprung der Olympischen Spiele', *Die Antike* 17 (1941), pp.189-208.

Meuli, K. *Der Griechische Agon*. Cologne, 1968.

Miall, D.S. (ed.) *Metaphor: Problems and Perspectives*. Brighton, 1982.

Motte, A. *Prairies et jardins dans la Grèce antique*. Brussels, 1971.

Moulinier, L. *Le Pur et l'impur dans la pensée des Grecs*. Paris, 1952.

Mugler, C. 'La lumière et la vision dans la poésie grecque', *REG* 73 (1960), pp.40-72.

Mühll, P. von der. 'Weitere pindarische Notizen', *MH* 25 (1968), pp.226-9.

Mullen, W. *Choreia: Pindar and Dance*. Princeton, 1982.

Nagy, G. *Comparative Studies in Greek and Indic Meter*. Cambridge, Mass., 1974.

Nagy, G. *The Best of the Achaeans*. Baltimore, 1979.

Nilsson, M.P. *The Minoan-Mycenaean religion and its survival in*

158   *Bibliography*

Greek religion. Lund, 1927.
Nilsson, M.P. 'The immortality of the soul in Greek religion', *Opuscula Selecta* vol.3. Lund, 1951-1960, pp.40-55.
Ninck, M. *Die Bedeutung des Wassers im Kult und Leben der Alten*. Repr. Darmstadt, 1960.
Nisbet, R.G.M. and Hubbard, M. *A Commentary on Horace: Odes Book I*. Oxford, 1970.
Nisetich, F.J. 'The leaves of triumph and mortality: transformation of a traditional image in Pindar's *Olympian 12*', *TAPA* 107 (1977), pp.235-64.
Nisetich, F.J. *Pindar's Victory Odes*. Baltimore, 1980.
Nowottny, W. *The Language Poets Use*. London, 1962, 1981.
Onians, R.B. *the Origins of European Thought about the Body, the Mind, the World, Time and Fate*. Cambridge, 1951.
Ortony, A. (ed.) *Metaphor and Thought*. Cambridge, 1979.
Otto, W.F. *Die Musen und der göttliche Ursprung des Singens und Sagens*. Darmstadt, 1956.
Parke, H.W. and Wormell, D.E.W. *The Delphic Oracle*. Oxford, 1956.
Parry, Adam. 'Landscape in Greek poetry', *YCS* 15 (1957), pp.3-29.
Parry, H. 'Ovid's *Metamorphoses*: violence in a pastoral landscape', *TAPA* 95 (1964), pp.268-82.
Parry, H. 'The second stasimon of Euripides' *Hippolytus*', *TAPA* 97 (1966), pp.317-26.
Péron, J. *Les Images maritimes de Pindare*. Paris, 1974.
Pfeiffer, R. (ed.) *Callimachus* 2 vols. Oxford, 1949, 1953.
Poliakoff, M. *Studies in the Terminology of the Greek Combat Sports*. Meisenheim, 1982.
Pollard, J. *Birds in Greek Life and Myth*. London, 1977.
Pucci, P. *Hesiod and the Language of Poetry*. Baltimore, London, 1971.
Ramnoux, C. *Héraclite, ou l'homme entre les choses et les mots*. Paris, 1959.
Richards, I.A. *The Philosophy of Rhetoric*. Oxford, 1936, 1979.
Ricoeur, P. *The Rule of Metaphor*. London, 1978.
Robert-Tornow, W. *De apium mellisque apud veteres significatione et symbolica et mythologica*. Berlin, 1893.
Robertson, D.S. 'The food of Achilles', *CR* 54 (1940), pp.177-80.
Rohde, E. *Psyche· Seelencult und Unsterblichkeitsglaube der Griechen*, trans. W.B. Hillis. New York, 1925/1950.
de Romilly, J. 'Gorgias et le pouvoir de la poésie', *JHS* 93 (1973), pp.155-62.
de Romilly, J. *Magic and Rhetoric in Ancient Greece*. Cambridge, Mass. and London, 1975.
Roscher, W.H. *Nektar und Ambrosia*. Leipzig, 1883.
Roscher, W.H. *Ausführliches Lexikon der griechischen und römischen Mythologie*. Leipzig, 1884-1937.
Rosenmeyer, T.G. *The Green Cabinet. Theocritus and the European Pastoral Lyric*. Berkeley and Los Angeles, 1969.

Russell, D.A. *'Longinus': On the Sublime*. Oxford, 1964.

Russell, D.A. and Winterbottom, M. *Ancient Literary Criticism*. Oxford, 1972.

de Saussure, F. *Cours de linguistique générale*, 5th ed. Paris, 1966, and in translation by R. Harris, London, 1983.

Schachermeyr, F. *Poseidon und die Entstehung des griechischen Götterglaubens* Bern, 1950.

Schadewaldt. W. *Der Aufbau des pindarischen Epinikion*. Halle, 1928.

Scheinberg, S. 'The bee maidens of the Homeric hymn to Hermes', *HSCP* 83 (1979), pp.1-24.

Schibles, W.A. *Metaphor: An Annotated Bibliography and History*. Wisconsin, 1971.

Schnapp-Gourbeillon, A. *Lions, héros, masques. Les représentations de l'animal chez Homère*. Paris, 1980.

Schofield, M. 'The dénouement of the *Cratylus*', in Schofield, M. and Nussbaum, M. (eds) *Language and Logos*. Cambridge, 1982, pp.61-81.

Séchan, L. *Le Mythe de Prométhée*. Paris, 1951.

Searle, J.R. 'Metaphor', in Ortony, A. (ed.), *Metaphor and Thought*. Cambridge, 1979, pp.92-123.

Segal, C.P. 'Gorgias and the psychology of the Logos', *HSCP* 66 (1962), pp.99-155.

Segal, C.P. 'God and man in Pindar's *First* and *Third Olympian Odes*', *HSCP* 68 (1964), pp.211-67.

Segal, C.P. 'Pindar's *7th Nemean*', *TAPA* 98 (1967), pp.431-80.

Segal, C.P. 'Horace *Odes* 2.6. Poetic landscape and poetic imagination', *Philologus* 113 (1969), pp.235-53.

Silk, M. *Interaction in Poetic Imagery*. Cambridge, 1974.

Simpson, M. 'The chariot and the bow as metaphors for poetry in Pindar's odes' , *TAPA* 100 (1969), pp.437-73.

Snell, B. *Die Entdeckung des Geistes. Studien zur Entstehung des europoaïschen Denkens bei den Griechen*, 3rd ed. Hamburg, 1955.

Soutar, G. *Nature in Greek Poetry*. London, 1939.

Stanford, W.B. *Greek Metaphor: Studies in Theory and Practice*. Oxford, 1936.

Stanford, W.B. *Ambiguity in Greek Literature*. Oxford, 1939.

Stern, G. *Meaning and Change of Meaning*. Gothenburg, 1931.

Stevens, Wallace. *The Collected Poems of Wallace Stevens*. New York, 1955.

Stinton, T.C.W. 'The riddle at Colonus', *GRBS* 17 (1976), pp.323-8.

Stoneman, R. 'The Theban eagle', *CQ* n.s. 26 (1976), pp.188-97.

Taillardat, J. *Les Images d'Aristophane*. Paris, 1965.

Tarrant, D. 'Greek metaphors of light', *CQ* 10 (1960), pp.181-7.

Thompson, D'Arcy Wentworth. *A Glossary of Greek Birds*, 2nd ed. London, 1936.

Todorov, T. *Littérature et signification*. Paris, 1967.

Treu, M. 'Licht und Leuchtendes in der archaischen griechischen

Poesie', *Studium Generale* 18 (1965), pp.83-97.
Tuan, Yi-Fu. *Landscapes of Fear*. Oxford, 1960.
Ullmann, S. *Language and Style*. Oxford, 1964.
Ullmann, S. *Semantics: An Introduction to the Science of Meaning*. Oxford, 1962, 1983.
Usener, H. 'Milch und Honig', *Kleine Schriften* 4. (Leipzig, Berlin, 1918).
Vermeule, E. *Aspects of Death in Early Greek Art and Poetry*. Berkeley and Los Angeles, 1979.
Vernant, J.-P. *Mythe et pensée chez les Grecs*. Paris, 1965.
Vernant, J.-P. *Mythe et société en Grèce ancienne*. Paris, 1974.
Vidal-Naquet, P. 'Plato's myth of the statesman; the ambiguities of the Golden Age and of history', *JHS* 98 (1978), pp.132-41.
Vidal-Naquet, P. 'Land and sacrifice in the *Odyssey*', in Gordon, R.L. (ed.), *Myth, Religion and Society*. Cambridge, 1981, pp.80-94.
Waszink, J.H. 'Biene und Honig als Symbol des Dichters und Dichtung in der griechischen-römischen Antike', *Rheinisch-Westfälische Akademie der Wisenschaften*, Vorträge G. (Opladen, 1974).
West, M. 'Near Eastern material in Hellenistic and Roman literature', *HSCP* 73 (1969), pp.113-34.
West, M. *Early Greek Philosophy and the Orient*. Oxford, 1971.
West, M. 'The Orphics of Olbia', *ZPE* 45 (1982), pp.17-28.
Wheelwright, P. *The Burning Fountain*. Bloomington, 1954.
Wheelwright, P. *Metaphor and Reality*. Bloomington, 1962.
White, K.D. *County Life in Classical Times*. London, 1977.
Wilamowitz-Moellendorff, U. von. *Der Glaube der Hellenen*, 2 vols. Berlin, 1931-1932.
Williams, B. 'Cratylus' theory of names and its refutation', in Schofield, M. and Nussbaum, M. *Language and Logos*. Cambridge, 1982, pp.83-94.
Wimsatt, W.K. with Beardsley, M.C. *The Verbal Icon*. Kentucky, 1954.
Woodbury, L. 'Equinox at Acragas: Pindar *Ol*.2.61-2', *TAPA* 97 (1966), pp.597-616.
Young, D.C. 'Pindaric criticism', *The Minnesota Review* 4 (1964), pp.584-641.
Young, D.C. *Three Odes of Pindar: A Literary Study of Pythian 11, Pythian 3 and Olympian 7*. Leyden, 1968.
Zuntz, G. *Persephone: Three Essays in Religion and Thought in Magna Graecia*. Oxford, 1971.

Index

Achilles, 63, 103, 140
Aeacus, Aeacidae, 80, 90
Aegina, 22, 67, 90, 115-16
Aelian, 106
Aeschylus: *Agamemnon*, quoted, 8, 32n, 69n; *Persae*, 13; *Prometheus Bound*, 56n
Aesop, 99
Aetna, Mount, 92, 95
Africa, 48, 67
Aglaia, 47, 49
Aglaurus, 46
agón, 112, 115; *see also* Games
Ajax, 140, 141, 143, 144
Alatheia, 47, 62n; *see also* truth
Alcaeus, 70
Alcimides, 80
Alcmaeon, 56
ambrosia, 129-30, 131
animals: Greek views of, 100-1; in metaphor, 13, 24, 99-110 *passim*; in myth, 102-3, 108-10
Antilochus, 138
aoidos, 52; *see also* poet
ape, 101
Aphrodite, 42, 110
Apollo, 43, 45, 94, 109, 139, 142; in cult, 92, 143; and poetry, 40, 108
Arcadia, 92
Arcesilus, 72
Archilochus, 70, 100
Ares, 7
Argo, Argonauts, 58, 109, 115
Arion, 106
Aristaeus, 43
Aristoteles, 80, 90

Aristotle, 5, 12; *Metaphysics*, quoted, 39n; *Poetics*, quoted, 6, 7, 8; *Rhetoric*, quoted, 3n, quoted, 7, 14, 16
Arrephoria, 46
arrival motif, 77
Artemis, 43, 49
Asclepius, 24-5, 56, 57, 131, 140
Asopodorus, 67
Athena, 60, 61
athlete, athletics: in cult, 112, 147; and dance, 83-4; in metaphor, 20, 58, 79, 111-21 *passim*; and war, 115-16; *see also* Games, poet-victor relationship
Auden, W.H., *The Fall of Rome*, quoted, 9

Bacchylides, 105n, 106n, 107, 113
Battus, 92
Baudelaire, C., 13, 75n
bee, 103, 106, 107, 109, 132
Benveniste, E., 6-7
birds, 12, 105-6, 107, 108-9, 132
Black, M., 7n, 8, 10n
Blake, W., 97; *A Poison Tree*, quoted, 11
blindness, 15, 82-3, 128
Boeotia, 43, 92
Boreas, Boreads, 69, 109
bow and arrow, as metaphor, 41, 108, 152
boxing, 113, 120
Breton, A., quoted, 9
breeze, as metaphor, 41, 68, 125; *see also* wind
building, as metaphor, 22, 55, 150

Cadmus, 45, 141
carpentry, as metaphor, 53, 56
Castalia, 45
Castor, 138
catachresis, 10
Centaurs, 102-3, 147
chariot, 124; of song, 41, 59, 79, 85
Cheiron, 94, 102-3
Chromius, 138
Cicero, *de oratore*, quoted, 5, 8, 13
clothing, as metaphor, 12, 59-60; *see also* weaving
Clytemnestra, 8
cock, 108
Coleridge, S.T., quoted, 38-9
Corinth, 74
crow, 102, 106
crown, crowning, 28, 36, 54, 90; as metaphor, 51, 53, 54, 64, 72, 114; *see also* wreath
cult, 42-3, 46, 92; and athletics, 112, 147
Cyrene, 48, 70, 92, 93, 94, 103, 142

daidalos, 60, 62-3
dance: among gods, 33, 40, 49, 152; Greek views of, 84, 119-20; of *kômos*, 53, 54, 66, 85
darkness, 47, 92; of death, 32, 128-9
de Saussure, F., 4
Delphi, 22, 45, 92, 109, 143
Demetrius, quoted, 7
dew, 46, 97
Diodotus, 32
Dionysus, 7, 43
Dirce, 45, 96
doctor, *see* medicine

eagle, 21, 102, 104, 105-6, 108, 109
Echo, 81
Elysium, 37, 125, 127
Empedocles, 56
encomium, *see* victory ode
Erato, 43
Ergoteles, 71, 115
Euadne, 94

Euphrosyne, 49

feasting, 20-1, 49, 50, 127
Field of Reeds, 130
Fontanier, P., 10
forgetfulness, 28, 82
fox, 101, 102
Fragment: **52a**, 30; **52f**, 57; **52h**, 117; **70a**, 35; **94b**, 72-3; **123**, 42, 57; **128**, 42; **128c**, 37; **129**, 38; **125**, 127; **171**, 32

Gadeira, 74, 93, 142
Gaia, 146
Games: origins, 60, 114, 132, 137-8; sites, 91; significance, 112-13
Garden of the Hesperides, 97n, 130
gardener, as metaphor, 37, 44, 97-8
gnome, 22-3, 25, 28, 68, 74, 139-40
gold, as metaphor, 38, 50, 126-7, 152
Golden Age, 37, 96-7, 100, 124, 126, 151
Gorgias, 16, 41n
Graces, 37, 40-51 *passim*, 52, 57, 62, 127, 130

Hades, 81, 92, 123, 127-9, 130, 134, 139
Hagesidamus, 46, 120
Hagesius, 108
Hecabe, 60
Heidegger, M., 39, 151n
Helicon, 43, 44, 45, 106, 150
helmsman, as metaphor, 7, 27, 58, 68-9, 70-1, 74-5; *see also* ship
Hephaistos, 61, 63
Hera, 102, 103
Heracles, 75, 80, 91, 95, 103, 114, 115, 138, 139, 141, 142, 146-7; Pillars of, 23, 71, 78, 95, 124, 141
herald, as metaphor, 52, 57, 77
Hermes, 44

Herodotus, 138
hero shrine, 60, 90, 115
Herse, 46
Hesiod, 76, 97, 100, 106, 122, 126;
  Theogony, 41, quoted, 43, 45,
  47, quoted, 73; *Works and
  Days*, quoted, 82, 83, 105n,
  quoted, 126, 127
Hesychia, 113
Hieron, 55, 73, 81, 92, 113, 118,
  125, 138
Hippolyte, 63
Homer, 14, 61, 67, 76, 107, 109,
  110, 122, 129; simile, 2, 100;
  Iliad, quoted, 29, 41, 53, 54, 60,
  63, quoted, 69, 83; *Odyssey*, 56,
  78, 125
honey, 97, 131; as metaphor, 45-6,
  103, 132, 133
Hora, Horae, 32, 37
horsemanship, 25, 58, 127
horses, 109-10
hospitality, *see xenia*
Hyperboreans, 38, 74, 95, 127, 140,
  141, 143

Iamos, 29, 30, 93, 94, 103, 116,
  143-4
iconography, 108; of death, 121,
  132-3
inspiration, 17, 37, 40, 41, 44-6,
  72-3
Iolaus, 138
Islands of the Blessed, 37, 38, 96,
  123, 127
Isthmian 1, 53, 67, 107, 138, 142; 2,
  62, 79, 82, 95; 3/4, 29, 32, 35, 47,
  58, 71, 83, 101; 5, 58, 70; 6, 41,
  45, 59, 96-7, 109; 7, 36, 72, 73,
  77, 117, 125, 126, 161; 8, 34,
  132, 133
Ixion, 102

Jason, 31, 94, 103, 109
javelin throwing, 104; as metaphor, 78, 113-14, 117

jumping, 104, as metaphor, 79,
  117

kairos, 58-9, 108
Keats, J., 15, 97; *Ode to Psyche*,
  quoted, 98
kleos, 35, 38, 41, 115, 122
kômos, 40, 49, 85, 115, 119-20; *see
  also* dance

lament, *see threnos*
language: ancient and modern
  theories of, 3-7; poetic, 10,
  14-16, 23, 38-9, 149-50, 152
Lévi-Strauss, C., 147
libations, as metaphor, 59, 131-2;
  see also melikraton
light, as metaphor, 13, 46-8, 50,
  82, 89, 116, 117, 128, 133-4, 150,
  152
lion, 101, 102
locus amoenus, 89
Lucian, 45

magic, magician, 56-7, 61
medicine, 56-7, 63; as metaphor,
  20, 24-5, 131
Melesias, 104
melikraton, 45, 132
Melissa, 45; *see also* bee
memory, *see* Mnemosyne
metaphor: definitions, 2, 5-6, 8-10;
  functions, 14-16, 18ff.; and
  myth, 136-7, 144ff.; theories,
  1-17 *passim*; types, 12-14, 19-21
Metis, 63
metonymy, 20
Metope, 45
Mimnermus, 29, 31
Mnemosyne, 41, 42, 47, 82
Moira, Moirae, 35
mule, 22, 106
Muse, Muses, 20, 38, 119, 120, 127,
  130, 150; and animals, 109; and
  craftsmanship, 54, 55-6, 62;
  and nature, 37, 42-9, 72, 73, 96;

and poet, 39-41, 59, 63, 78, 106, 108, 116-17, 152; and victory celebration, 49-50

myth, 91-2, 94, 95, 112, 115, 137-8; animals in, 102-3, 108-10; and death, 127-31; and metaphor, 136-7, 144-8; and victors' ancestors, 80, 90-1

naming complex, 89

navigation, as metaphor, 73-4, 109; *see also* helmsman

nectar, 45, 72, 129-30, 131

Nemean 1, 47, 48, 90, 138; **2**, 8; **3**, 21, 22, 23, 47, 63, 69, 71, 73, 75, 77, 80, 103, 105-6, 108, 115, 129, 132; **4**, 20, 22, 24, 30, 46, 56, 64, 68, 77, 79, 93, 114, 117, 118, 119, 120, 132; **5**, 20, 22, 49, 50, 58, 60, 63, 73, 74, 79, 85, 90, 104, 106, 115, 117, 134, 139; **6**, 22, 29, 33, 41, 67, 77, 79-80, 104; **7**, 24, 25, 47, 50, 54, 72, 77, 82, 107, 113, 116, 117, 119, 128, 140, 141, 143; **8**, 21, 36, 46, 55, 60, 64, 132, 139, 140, 141, 144; **9**, 21, 30, 50, 70, 89-90, 117, 119, 128; **11**, 33, 113

Neoptolemus, 140, 143

Nereid, 43

Nestor, 138

night, as metaphor, 67; *see also* darkness

nightingale, 105, 107

Nymphs, 34, 43, 46, 130; and inspiration, 44-5; reception of victor, 48-9

Odysseus, 56, 61

Oenomaus, 45

oimê, 78-9; *see also* path

Olympia, Olympic Games, 19-20, 91, 104-5, 114, 115, 127

Olympus, Mount, 41, 125

Olympian 1, 20, 25, 30, 38, 54n, 57, 60, 62, 81, 85, 90-1, 93, 115, 119, 125-6, 131, 134, 138, 143; **2**, 29, 34, 37, 50, 63, 69, 102, 116, 125, 126, 127; **3**, 25, 53, 56, 83, 91, 114; **4**, 26, 33, 37, 63; **5**, 90, 113; **6**, 22, 29, 30, 32, 37, 53, 55, 60, 67, 82, 84, 92, 93, 94, 103, 106, 108, 113, 117, 127; **7**, 20, 29-30, 30n, 35, 41, 42, 45, 48, 50, 56, 68, 82, 83, 130; **8**, 79, 114, 117; **9**, 37, 41, 44, 47, 63, 72, 78, 79, 85, 118, 139; **10**, 42, 46, 47, 72, 91, 114, 120, 129, 130; **11**, 101, 102; **12**, 68, 71, 108, 115, 140; **13**, 68, 73, 74, 77, 117; **14**, 36, 42, 47, 49, 81, 127, 128

Orchomenos, 42

Orestes, 143

Orpheus, 44, 106

Ortygia, 118

Ouranos, 146

Paean, 37

Pan, 44, 49, 106

Pandora, 146

Pandrosus, 46

Parmenides, 78

path, as metaphor, 22, 76-7, 78-85 *passim*

Pausanias, 44-5, 96

Pegasus, 110

Pelias, 31

Pelops, 30, 92, 93, 115, 116, 134, 138, 140, 143

Persephone, 81, 129

Perseus, 74, 95, 140, 141

Persuasion, 42, 57

phyllobolia, 36, 107-8

plant, as metaphor, 21, 28-39 *passim*, 68, 126-7, 150

Plato, 146, 151; *Cratylus*, 3, 4; *Gorgias*, 63; *Ion*, 16; *Laws*; 83, quoted, 84, 119; *Republic*, 112

ploughman, as metaphor, 37, 44

poet: initiation, 44, 45; role, 35-6, 53-4, 72, 77, 135; skills, 41, 61, 63, 116-17; status, 62

poet-victor relationship, 28-9, 73, 78-9, 105, 117-18
poikilos, 60, 62-3
Poseidon, 37, 93, 109, 110, 134, 139, 144
Prometheus, 61, 146
prophecy, prophet, as metaphor, 45, 57, 103, 109
Psaumis, 90
psyche, 123
Pythagoreans, 101, 136
Pythia, 109
Pythian 1, 20, 46, 49, 54, 55, 56, 57, 70, 92, 95, 104, 109, 113, 114, 117, 141; **2**, 19, 24, 26, 48, 83, 101, 118; **3**, 20, 31, 24, 38, 49, 53, 57, 73, 127, 131, 140; **4**, 31, 34, 41, 58, 68, 109, 115, 130; **5**, 46, 56, 60, 72, 80, 81, 90, 94; **6**, 22, 37, 44, 45, 59, 65, 138; **7**, 55; **8**, 23, 31, 36, 77, 113, 128; **9**, 48, 70, 93, 94, 108, 142; **10**, 26, 38, 71, 74-5, 81, 106, 107, 140, 141, 143; **11**, 73, 85, 143; **12**, 48, 140

rhetoric, 14, 16, 17, 61n, 63, 145
Rhodes, 29, 48, 82
Richards, I.A., 2n, 8
Ricoeur, P., 5n, 8, 10n, 152n
ring composition, 25, 85
rites, 30, 33, 131-4
roots, as metaphor, 34-5

Sappho, 2, 31
Sarpedon, 69
sculpture, 20, 22, 44
sea, 58, 92-3, 95; and inspiration, 72-3; and poet, 73-4; as symbol, 67-8
Seasons, 40; *see also* Hora, Horae
Semonides, 13, 29, 100
Shakespeare, W., *Antony and Cleopatra*, quoted, 8; *King Lear*, 12; *Richard II*, 10; *Twelfth Night*, quoted, 13
Shelley, P.B., quoted, 5-6
ship: of life, 70, 71; of song, 73-4;

of state, 7, 20, 70-1
shipwreck, as metaphor, 67
Sicily, 67, 92
simile, 7; *see also* Homer
snake, 103
Sogenes, 116
soma, 130
sophia, 41, 44, 63
Sophocles, *Oedipus Rex*, 15
Sparta, Spartans, 57, 92, 111
spring, 43, 44, 45; as metaphor, 130, 96-7
stêlê, 64, 132
Stevens, W., *The Man with the Blue Guitar*, quoted, 15
storm, as metaphor, 32, 70
Strepsiades, 72
Stymphalus, 92
sun, sunlight, 124-5; as metaphor, 10, 30, 72, 89
Syracuse, 92
synaesthesia, 13

Tantalus, 131, 138, 143
Telescrates, 93
Thalia, *thalia*, 35, 49
Thanatos, 128
Thebes, 45, 92
Theia, 58
Theognis, 70
thesauros, 59
Thetis, 49
Thrasybulus, 138
threnos, 133-4
thumos, 69, 107
Timodemus, 80
tomb, 60, 64, 131; *see also* hero shrine
transitions, 24-6, 75, 84-5, 142
tree, as metaphor, 23, 32, 34, 46
truth, 42, 47, 120; *see also* Alatheia
Tuche, 71
Typhon, 95, 141

Underworld, 12, 14; *see also* Hades

victory list, 21
victory ode, 18ff., 28, 60, 138; components, 21, 22; structure, 24, 61, 74-5, 84-5, 120, 142; range of material, 22-3, 34, 91, 136, 138

water, 19, 24; and inspiration, 44-5, 72-3; of life and death, 129-31; and poetry, 46
weather, as metaphor, 32, 69-70, 72, 89, 125-6
weaving, as metaphor, 54, 63
welding, as metaphor, 54-5
wind: and death, 68, 124; and inspiration, 73; and mortal fortunes, 21, 68-70, 78; and poetry, 73
wine, as metaphor, 20, 50, 119, 132

wings, 132-3; and words, 13, 107
wolf, 83, 101
wreath, 30, 133; as metaphor, 20, 36, 37, 38, 48, 50-1, 64, 107, 108, 114, 118; *see also* crown, crowning
wrestling, 49; as metaphor, 24, 113, 117-18, 120; and dance, 119

Xanthus, 110
xenia, 77, 90, 95, 119
Xenophanes, 78

yoking, as metaphor, 53

Zephyrs, 125
Zeus, 43, 49, 59, 95, 102, 104, 109, 146